Contents

PREFACE

Talk about a dinner party! Imagine these people all sitting at a table — what a fascinating dozen people to talk to. They were there when it all happened. Each can tell amazing stories about kindness and love. If we push them, they can remember some horrible cruelty and petty vindictiveness.

The first people to lead the church came from a smorgasbord of backgrounds. They were tent-makers, fishermen, widows, Pharisees, Gentiles, Jews. They tried to melt into one pot, but sometimes they were a strange mixture. Tempers could still boil, racism could raise its ugly frame, and some could fail to forgive.

But whether they were in a king's palace or a prison's chains, they had one thing in common: Each lived, sacrificed and was willing to die for Jesus Christ.

While you read these chapters I hope you can imagine each one sitting at the table. Look into their eyes as they recount those pioneer years. Listen carefully when they tell you how good God is in the living Christ.

William L. Coleman
Aurora, Nebraska

1
BARNABAS

He Saw the Best in Everyone

Nicknames are popular with children. When I was a child, there was one friend at our local playground called "Big Ears." I knew him for two years and never learned his real name. He will always be Big Ears to me. Usually we earned our new names by something strange about us: Curly, Pokey or even Fats.

Barnabas was an early Christian who picked up a nickname by being kind. His parents, who lived in Cyprus, named their son Joseph. But he was such a considerate and generous person that his Christian friends called him Barnabas. It meant "Son of Encouragement," and fit him exactly. Barnabas was a Levite from the priestly family of Jews.

We don't have the details of his conversion, but, since he had relatives living in Jerusalem, he may have been visiting them when he became a Christian. Large numbers of dispersed Jews had returned to Jerusalem to celebrate Pentecost. He may have heard about Christ during this time and decided not to return to Cyprus.

Luke, the author, seems particularly proud of this convert. He introduces him in Acts 4:36, probably as a commentary on Christian sharing.

Some of the difficulties which those early Christians faced must have been dramatically emotional. Many had been estranged from their families because of their new faith. Both Gentiles and Jews found it hard to see their relatives embrace a crucified Nazarene.

A number of others collided abruptly with financial disaster. Some were instantly fired from their jobs as their Christian conversion became known. This practice was to plague new believers for years. Young people who believed in the resurrection could be thrown out of their homes without income or jobs.

So, the collection of believers took the obligation of support on their own shoulders. They immediately adopted each other and worked together to solve their problems. Each became engulfed in the warm, accepting arms of those who could help. The church Barnabas worshiped with was tender, loving and concerned. A brother's need became everyone's problem.

It was a cosmopolitan congregation. Those of economic privilege were interwoven with slaves and laborers. They blended into a beautiful pattern. It is easy to imagine some believers who had always been poor. They had menial trades or possibly slave status. Their economy did not change with their new faith. It was always desperate.

As the church grew and spread, its concerns remained the same. It alleviated the financial vice which squeezed so many. Help was directed toward widows who had no support. It found its way to famine-stricken areas and on occasion enabled a dedicated missionary to travel across the continent. This humanitarian practice presented problems, but the early church refused to shy from its opportunity.

Barnabas owned a piece of land and was one of the first disciples to respond to the church's needs by selling his property and contributing the money. He could have kept it; Christianity did not demand his possessions. It merely offered a channel to sacrificing people for them to share what they had. Barnabas responded to the challenge instantly. He did not choose to be encumbered by the responsibilities of property. The money would be needed in supporting new believers who were bent on living for the resurrected Christ.

In just two verses (verses 36, 37), Luke gives a pithy, arresting introduction to the Son of Encouragement. It is a hint of Barnabas' gigantic supply of kindness and generosity.

As Acts opens, another nickname becomes obvious for Barnabas. He could have been called "Son Of One Who Sticks His Neck Out." For an infamous convert named Paul, for a tragedy-stricken church, and for a rejected apostle named Mark, Barnabas became daring, patient and loving. He set a standard which the church has admired for centuries.

The first church never enjoyed the luxury of peace. From day one their antagonists lined up, stones in hand and hate in their eyes. After Stephen was killed by a hostile crowd, Christians poured out of Jerusalem for their own safety (Acts 8). The only Christians who remained in the sacred city were the ones designated "apostles." Barnabas' reputation had mushroomed so quickly that he was considered an apostle. He remained in the city which was now his home.

The pressure on local Christians must have been enormous. Those who stayed ran constant risks; men and women were being arrested almost daily. They were torn from their homes and incarcerated. More deaths were certain to follow. Men such as the dreaded Saul of Tarsus were leading a merciless campaign against people who believed in the resurrection of Jesus.

Barnabas crossed the path of Saul (who was also called Paul) in an unusual way. After Paul's spectacular conversion (Acts 9), he attempted to contact and join the Christian apostles. Their enthusiasm was less than boundless.

The very name of the man caused Christians to shake. God directly asked Ananias to minister to the former persecutor, and the man of God balked. How could anyone trust the giant net who dragged everyone to prison? Ananias finally relented and went to help the struggling new believer.

Paul faced a monumental pressure in his new faith. The Jews sought to kill him for turning to Jesus Christ. He finally had to escape Damascus and travel to Jerusalem. When he tried to contact the disciples there, they shrugged him off like a duck throwing water.

But somehow Paul met the Son of Encouragement. Barnabas stuck his neck out. If this was some bizarre conspiracy, the apostles could pay with their lives. Yet there was no way for Barnabas to escape personal responsibility, and he decided to become a mediator. He had heard of someone else who had been *his* Mediator.

Barnabas described Paul's conversion to the apostles and outlined the preaching ministry which had followed.

That meeting between the disciples and Paul and Barnabas had to be one of the most significant conferences in history. We can only speculate what would have happened if the apostles had turned Paul out that day. What would it have done to his personal faith? How would it have affected the path of Christianity?

What we do know is that Barnabas decided to turn the key, opening the door to Paul. History will always treat Paul as one of the great leaders of Christianity and the world. But those who read the book of Acts know the story behind it. Barnabas allowed the famous apostle to stand on his shoulders.

There appears to be a steady quality about Barnabas. He is willing to give all he has and take huge personal risks. Yet, he doesn't seem to mind being number two.

Relative peace followed the conversion of Paul, especially in outlying areas of Jerusalem. It seems no accident for Luke to make a note about peace at this point (Acts 9:31). He has just discussed the conversion and incorporation of the chief persecutor. His force had accounted for the major thrust of antagonism during these early years.

If anyone doubts that one man could have this much impact on the church, consider the later facts. After his conversion Paul became the great leader of Christianity—bar none. It would be difficult to exaggerate Paul's natural and spiritual prowess.

The gospel spread rapidly and people responded.

Phoenicia, Cyprus and Antioch heard the good news and soon collections of believers were formed (Acts 11:19, 20). When news came back to Jerusalem concerning the converts, the apostles jumped for joy. They met in session and decided to send Barnabas to Antioch to teach the new believers and help their faith grow.

Barnabas never blinked an eye. He caught the next pair of sandals out of town. And what was the first thing he did when he arrived at Antioch? He "encouraged" them. What else would the courageous Son of Encouragement do?

Not only did Barnabas function as a teacher, but he was a first-class evangelist. Many people came to understand and accept the death and resurrection of Jesus Christ through Barnabas' ministry.

It was typical of the apostle to continually think of other people. His thoughts soon scanned to his friend, Paul. He wondered what kind of ministry was claiming his talents. Barnabas took off for Tarsus and asked Paul to come join him in Antioch. There was a lot to do: teaching, preaching and praying for a young and enthused congregation.

Paul consented and soon they again stood shoulder to shoulder. They spent one year at Antioch and watched God perform miracles. The word *Christian* crystalized here, and for the first time believers began to wear this title.

During their stay in Antioch an unexpected opportunity came for the Christians to show kindness. Some prophets from Jerusalem came to visit them and made a startling prediction. Agabus prophesied a terrible famine which would sweep across the entire Roman Empire.

It is easy, within a ten-year period, to mark the time of this calamity. Claudius was emperor from A.D. 41-54. During his reign a series of dearths stretched across the empire. Many bad harvests and famines kept the populace in dire straits. The entire land was probably never locked in at once; rather, a series of terrible setbacks continuously swept across the land.

The Christians responded rapidly to the imminent crisis. They had learned well the principles of sharing. There was no better teacher than Barnabas who divested himself completely to follow Christ.

Each person gave "according to his ability" (Acts 11:29). No pressure. No prejudice. No discrimination. The feeling was fresh and fun. The concern was genuine.

When they had collected what they could, emissaries had to be appointed to make the delivery. Barnabas and Paul were singled out to carry the shipment of love. It is probably safe to assume the gift was in the form of money. Years later Paul remembered the lesson and encouraged the church at Corinth to do the same thing (I Corinthians 16:1 ff).

Barnabas and Paul completed their mission to Jerusalem and returned to Antioch (Acts 12:25). This time they had with them a man named John who was called Mark. This person would later become a point of contention between the famous partners. Mark may have been a cousin to Barnabas (Colossians 4:10).

The people at Antioch had learned to greatly love both Barnabas and his friend Paul. The power of God was obvious as their ministry continued to reach many. The local church now had fine, qualified teachers and, rather than become complacent, the partners' eyes started looking to faraway lands again.

One day while the local congregation was worshiping God and fasting, the Holy Spirit communicated with them (Acts 13:2). We can't be sure how the Spirit accomplished this. Any number of avenues were open. The more important fact is the willingness of the Christians to accept this communication. The message was to send Barnabas and Paul on a missionary journey. Obediently, even cheerfully, they laid their hands on the pair and sent them on a great adventure.

The practice of laying on hands has a rich heritage in the Bible. Jacob began the ritual (Genesis 48:14) and Jesus honored it (Matthew 19:15). It was often incorporated in healing ministries. In the early church, hands were associated with spiritual gifts (Acts 8:15-18; 19:6). Timothy was instructed to live up to the gift conferred on him by the laying on of hands (I Timothy 4:14).

Today Christians in various denominations still use the ceremony on special occasions. It is often associated with ordination services. Someone once mused it is the laying of empty hands on empty heads. However, the service held deep significance for Barnabas and Saul.

Their companion on the journey was again the able young Mark. He was to share in amazing adventures along the way, as they did not lack excitement. In Paphos, a Jewish sorcerer named Elymas tried to stop their ministry. Paul called him down and partial blindness overcame the troublemaker.

In Pisidian Antioch Paul preached in the

synagogue and created a great stir. Many Jews wanted to discuss Jesus, and the missionaries were invited back on the next Sabbath. Not only were Jews converted but also many Gentiles turned to Christ. In fact, they created so much stir they were forced out of the city and region.

Undaunted, Barnabas and company traveled to Iconium. Many people heard them with favor, yet others did not. They soon left town, chased by flying stones.

At Lystra the team was also successful (Acts 14:6 ff), so successful that after they had healed a cripple the crowd confused them with gods and wanted to offer sacrifices to them. Before long, however, Jews from past congregations in Antioch and Iconium persuaded the multitudes at Lystra to stone Paul, since he was the principal speaker. He was stoned, but arose, and the next day Paul, Barnabas and Mark probably had mixed emotions as they departed for Derbe.

When they arrived back at Antioch they gathered the Christians for a special report. Many cities had been visited. Converts had been won, churches had been organized and vital teaching was going on. God had opened the door of the faith not only to the Jews but now directly to the Gentiles.

Barnabas had helped play the bridge again; he was a minister of reconciliation. Now God had a gigantic role for him to fulfill. A council had been called at Jerusalem to determine one of the greatest questions ever to face the church (Acts 15). Briefly put, many Jewish Christians resented Gentiles coming directly into the church. They felt they must first become Jews by being circumcised. Then they could become

Christians.

As absurd as this argument sounds to us, their logic was not groundless. They insisted that the Old Testament was still alive; therefore, the rules had to be kept.

What they did not understand was that the old law had been replaced by the new (Colossians 2:9-23). Now, *all* people needed to know that the door was directly open to Jesus Christ for anyone. If this argument was lost, Christianity would become merely another Jewish sect.

When the time came for Barnabas and Paul to testify before the council, the crowd was as quiet as cotton. The partners told the audience what they had seen God do among the Gentiles. They were being converted; they were growing; they were maturing and sending out missionaries. How could the church at Jerusalem throw cold water on these growing congregations? How could they demand Gentiles become Jews?

The day was won. The council agreed to send the message out. Tell the Gentiles to abstain from food polluted by idols, from sexual immorality and from meat of strangled animals when the blood has not been properly drained. Try your best not to offend the Jews who maintain these laws; but don't worry about becoming one. You are welcome to the church of Jesus Christ.

And who was going to go and tell the happy decision to the Gentiles? Who else? Barnabas and Paul were too good to turn down. They gathered Barsabas and Silas and were on their way.

Barnabas' ministry was essentially encouragement and reconciliation. But even the great apostle could not mollify everybody. Eventually the day would come when he and his close brother, Paul, simply could not agree.

The issue which wounded them centered on a man we met earlier—John Mark. We were introduced to Mark when Barnabas and Paul brought him back from Jerusalem. On their first missionary venture, Mark traveled along as an assistant. But when they left Paphos for Perga in Pamphylia Mark decided to return to Jerusalem (Acts 13:13).

The reason why he left is not spelled out by the author. Possibly Luke is being gracious. However, he is firm enough to include the debate between Paul and Barnabas. Whatever the reason for the departure, Paul is clearly upset. He felt so strongly he refused to take Mark along on this journey.

Barnabas and Paul decided to separate because their disagreement was "sharp" (Acts 15:39). It was not a misunderstanding or a personality conflict. They were not whimpering over some misguided insults. There was no bitter exchange between the steady friends, but their differences of opinion were clearly drawn.

The Son of Encouragement decided to stick his neck out again. Paul felt he could no longer depend on Mark and the apostle may have been correct. We don't know why Mark left; his reasoning may have been immature. But Barnabas was also correct. He was going to give his cousin a second chance.

Barnabas gathered Mark into his nest and they headed for Cyprus to spread the gospel. We can only guess what would have happened if Mark had been rejected. It could have made him stronger—or he may have withered.

We do believe he is the same Mark who went on to write the second Gospel. He was later reconciled with Paul (Colossians 4:10; Philemon 24), and joined him as an assistant in the ministry. Paul learned to trust him and sent Mark to help instruct Timothy (II Timothy 4:11).

Barnabas had again become a bridge. Mark used him to continue his service as a missionary.

There probably were times when Barnabas stuck his neck out and got stepped on. If so, Luke omits those tales. But he does paint a daring Christian who wasn't afraid to take a chance for other people.

Something To Think About

1. What does the early church teach us about sharing possessions?

2. Does your local church serve a mixture of people or is it basically one social level? Is this good or bad?

3. Do modern Christians stick their necks out for "questionable" characters? Explain.

4. Are waiting periods for baptism and membership good and helpful? Why or why not?

5. How does the relief program work in your church? Does it help individuals, congregations or nations? What can we learn from Antioch's example?

6. Describe the situation at the Jerusalem Council. Are local churches now open to all races and nationalities?

7. What does Barnabas' example teach us about giving a person a second chance? Is this attitude evident among the Christians you know?

2
STEPHEN

He Lived the Spirit of Christ

In a creative writing class, a fifth grade boy wrote a sentence about a certain nationality. His hate for this ethnic group was startling. It was especially disturbing because he had probably never met one person from that country.

Often our prejudices run deep long after we have forgotten how they started. The first church in Jerusalem suffered from the same uneasiness. Early converts came from varied ethnic backgrounds, and sometimes their buried prejudices wiggled to the top.

Sometimes we forget how successful the Israelites were at evangelism. The Pharisees were especially dedicated to converting pagans throughout the Roman world. Jesus gave them a backhanded compliment on their zealousness (Matthew 23:15).

Many Greeks were tired of the dry philosophical approach to God. Romans were often disgusted with emperors who claimed to be deity. Their drunken excesses and bloodthirstiness left thousands empty and searching.

Stephen, born a Greek, was one of the thousands who converted to Judaism during this time. Greek Jews were often called "Hellenists" by Jewish nationals. During the observance of Pentecost, Hellenists traveled great distances to worship in Israel. When they heard the gospel of the risen Christ, many responded and became Christians. Somehow, Stephen became a Christian. Other than this, we know nothing about Stephen's early life.

It was easy to embrace Christianity at first. The freshness and fellowship reached out like a mother's arms on a cold day. But after a time the newness wore off and the rough edges of ethnic differences started to rub raw. Tolerance gave way to impatience while zeal sank to hard realities.

The first serious ethnic rift started over the noblest of causes. Christians had devised a system to help take care of widows. It was a natural service for any group with a Jewish heritage. Their concern for widows was compassionate and guaranteed by God (Malachi 3:5). The New Testament church took up this responsibility with enthusiasm (I Timothy 5:3, 9; James 1:27).

It would be hard to guess how the problem started; there is no way to be sure if the situation was exaggerated. However, we can be certain prejudice and distrust were at the bottom of the aggravation.

The Greeks made the charge against the Hebrews: Greek widows were being neglected financially. Evidently the Jewish nationals were handling the widows' fund and its distribution. Somehow, well-meaning men with serious concern were allowing their feelings to shred an otherwise loving situation.

Some of us can remember when modern Christians have tripped on the same ethnic blindness. When I was a teenager in Washington, D.C., three black children were put out of our church. An aggressive teacher had brought three of the neighborhood youth to Vacation Bible School, and within ten minutes the trio was escorted back outside. The dedicated teacher was warned not to be a troublemaker.

When the twelve apostles heard of the friction, they wisely decided to get others to handle it. Their suggestion was to appoint seven men with high spiritual qualifications. Each man should have three basic assets: He must be well thought of, be controlled by the Holy Spirit, and give evidence of wisdom. Simple, rock-bottom Christian living. Later the guidelines would be amplified to include other virtues and restrictions (I Timothy 3:8 ff).

These honored seven became the first church deacons. In different denominations and groups the office assumes an array of responsibilities. The word deacon simply means "to serve." These deacons met a specific need for the early Christians. Their contributions both prevented a potential volcano and helped a needy group of believers.

The deacon decision catapulted Stephen into a leadership possibility. Of the seven designated, he was named first. His qualifications were established and solid. Christian zeal vibrated through his system.

Now he had a job, an office, a title. But he also knew there was no need to departmentalize his Christian life. He considered himself first of all a general Christian.

Sometimes discussions of spiritual gifts tend to

pigeonhole our thinking. Because of our self-imagined fences, there are many adventures we may never try. We see ourselves as one-legged, one-winged birds. And anybody knows a creature that limited had better be careful where he flies.

Self image has a great deal to do with how we perform. If I see myself as non-creative, it is certainly true. If I picture myself as having nothing to offer, then I don't and won't.

Call someone average and he will probably believe it—and live up to it. Tell someone he isn't executive material and he may stop dreaming. Raise a child to think he is inferior and he may well become a fizzle.

They called Stephen a deacon and he appreciated it. After all, it was an honor. But they didn't try to tell him he couldn't do other things, too. He wanted a full, multicolor, adventuresome Christian life. He would distribute gifts with enthusiasm, but he would also sample the other varieties of Christian service along the way.

Once the deacons were watching over the affairs of the church, the Christians were no longer draining their energies fighting each other. There was harmony, and great numbers were deciding to become Christians (Acts 6:7).

Stephen was an instrument in these events. Something wonderful had touched his life and he was moving like a politician in October. Anyone who would stand still was going to hear what Christ had done in his life.

His zeal soon led him to a synagogue in Jerusalem. The city had plenty of houses of worship, but this one was special because it was a synagogue especially for former slaves. Called Libertines, they once lived in

Cyrene, Alexandria, Cilicia and Asia. They were Hellenistic Jews like Stephen himself. A natural place for the new deacon to preach.

There was no difficulty getting to speak in the synagogue. Traveling teachers were often invited to address the assembly (Acts 13:14 ff). It was also common for men to stand up, to object to a speaker's comments. Their interruptions were pointed and often aggressive. Good speakers like Stephen looked forward to the exchange and came well-armed with ironclad evidence.

It is possible Saul of Tarsus sat in the congregation to hear Stephen. This would certainly explain his later involvement in Stephen's death (Acts 8:1).

Synagogues were not always the placid, dull dwellings we normally picture. Sometimes people prayed with loud, exaggerated forms. They were not disorderly, nor were they solemn and rigid.

It is safe to assume the content of the debate. Stephen was wound up by his new belief in a risen Messiah. Convinced and articulate, he was ready to take on the corridors of scholarship.

Luke, the careful historian, tells us how the battle went. Members of the congregation offered counterpoints and protests, but to no avail. For each objection Stephen responded with Old Testament wisdom and logic. (There is nothing wrong with incorporating both, as Saul himself would later do.)

Did Stephen cross the threshold of propriety? Was he too insulting and outlandish in his presentation? Luke, the author, doesn't criticize him in the least. Therefore we can feel assured that the congregation's strong hostility was centered on his doctrine and not on his personality. Stephen was not charged with ill manners. He was in the correct setting and his decorum was sound. If the crowd was offended by his message, it was not Stephen's fault.

I can remember one young man bragging about the persecution he faced. To hear him tell it, people disliked him because of Jesus Christ. The fact was, most could not stand him because of his obnoxious personality. They didn't necessarily understand what he was talking about, but they were sure they didn't want it. A difficult fact to get across to any zealot.

In Stephen's case, the opposition does not come across as kindly. Unable to out-argue or defeat his logic, they collected informers to testify against Stephen. Some of these witnesses were asked to lie before the council, just as similar testimonies had been assembled against Jesus (Matthew 26:59, 60). When they started to spread the story around, it assumed wild proportions. His detractors charged Stephen with blasphemy, not only against Moses but God.

Moses has always served as a security blanket. Anyone who wanted to sound pious could latch on to the ancient patriarch's name. It's similar to Republicans grabbing for Lincoln or Democrats extoling Jackson as their half brother.

The incensed mob claimed Stephen was an enemy of Moses. The desert leader would cringe if he could hear how his name is tossed about. They accused Stephen of speaking against the temple and the law. It was the same worn charge leveled against Jesus not long before that — the claim that Jesus of Nazareth would destroy the temple. These false witnesses flunked originality.

Acts 6:11-14 would be a good passage for every

Christian to read each day before breakfast. Then we should spend the next twelve hours being careful of what we say about others. It is easy to distort a few comments to unbearable proportions, and to stretch and disfigure a person's remark is a heinous crime. We should all be made to suck sour lemons.

The Sanhedrin council grimaced as they listened to the charges. It was indeed a serious matter. They shook their heads and scratched their beards. Their shock was clearly incurable. They found the false witnesses easy to believe because they wanted to.

We can't be sure what kind of expression settled on Stephen's face. We do know it made the audience think of an angel (6:15). We also are sure it contrasted the faces dotting the Sanhedrin. On one side were the angry and insecure. They were trying to decide whether to kill again. The other side sat peacefully, fully aware of who Stephen was and where he stood.

Caiaphas, the high priest, listened to the proceedings. The entire situation had to bring back horrible memories for him. Not so long before, he had condemned Jesus of Nazareth in this same room. That had been supposed to end this Christian thing. But to his bewilderment, Jesus' body was gone and this little cult was growing.

Maybe he would have to kill again. And maybe again—he was determined to snuff out this sect no matter how much blood was spilled. After listening, Caiaphas took charge as he had done at the trial of Jesus, and asked Stephen if these charges were true.

Not noted for his bashfulness, the sparky deacon jumped at the chance to reply. It looked to him like a good opportunity to explain his position, and he decided to teach Jewish history in the same course. It took Luke considerable space to record the remarkable speech (Acts 7:1-53). Even at that, he probably left large sections out.

There was a solid purpose to Stephen's Old Testament outline. His illustrations of God's working were germane to his defense. In essence, he was being accused of saying God could get along without the temple. His reply was that God isn't dependent on the building.

His argument showed that Abraham, Jacob, Joseph and even Moses met with God without benefit of a permanent structure. His speech peaks in Acts 7:48, 49: "Howbeit the most High dwelleth not in temples made with hands; as saith the prophet, Heaven is my throne, and earth is my footstool: what house will ye build me? saith the Lord: or what is the place of my rest?"

What accusation was Stephen leveling? That their worship of God had become cemented. They wanted no new information from heaven. There was no doubt what God was like, what He wanted or even where He lived. The gates to their minds were locked and the keys long ago had been dropped into the Dead Sea.

The Jewish leaders had committed religious suicide. They had lost their humility, and if it couldn't be recaptured, such cases were usually terminal.

There was once a church which suffered the same disease. The church began in a small frame building with a handful of believers. The congregation grew rapidly. Soon the walls were lined with people. New converts listened with eager hearts.

Observers in the community complimented them on the evident miracle. The pastor praised them for the hard work and dedication. Soon the congregation started to believe all they heard. They began patting themselves on the back.

It wasn't long before they lost their humility. After all, they were the prize evangelicals of the area. When they became convinced of their own beauty they soon turned to bickering among themselves. Nit-picking and Pharisaism took place. They stopped growing and merely sputtered. Five different camps played tug-of-war against each other. Consumed by pride, they drowned in their own arrogance.

Stephen was suggesting that the same thing had happened to the Sanhedrin. Void of humility, they were rigid and brittle in the hands of God. The bouncy deacon didn't want them to miss this point, so he aimed it carefully.

He had been quoting from Isaiah 66:1, but now he decided to free-lance. Beginning with Acts 7:51, he gives his own editorial comment. Stephen calls his audience "stiffnecked and uncircumcised"—two descriptives which they couldn't ignore. They considered themselves open to the bidding of God, and certainly they were circumcised.

We can debate the tact used by Stephen, for early Christians were no more infallible than the current crop. But Luke didn't attack Stephen's message or his approach. The Sanhedrin had continued to be hardheaded. They were not impressed with Jesus and voted to condemn him. There was no reason for Stephen to believe they would blossom into the welcome wagon for one of Jesus' disciples.

There comes a time to deliver the truth bluntly,

and Stephen determined this was the hour. He wasn't too far off base. His accusations were identical to those leveled by Jesus Christ: "Which of the prophets have not your fathers persecuted?" (Acts 7:52a; Matthew 23:37).

In all fairness to the Sanhedrin, the charge had to be shocking. All those years they thought they had been on the side of the prophets. They were difficult words to deliver or receive gracefully.

But the problem of humility arises again. How can we be confident and humble at the same time? A neat trick, but absolutely essential. A follower of Christ has to know what he believes (II Timothy 1:12). Yet he must also be open and flexible.

Too often we want to be taught what we already know. There is comfort in rehearsing the familiar. We are too often afraid to learn anything new. We sometimes consider it a sin to change our minds. This lack of openness qualifies us for the twentieth century Sanhedrin.

To put it mildly, Stephen wasn't endeared to his audience by his remarks. Luke's language is graphic. Their hearts were sawed in half. All of us can identify—we think our heart has been broken; theirs were cut through the center.

The gnashing of teeth is more difficult to understand. Some highly capable commentators believe the members literally jumped on him and started biting his flesh. However, a better explanation may be merely grinding their teeth. Teeth grinding was an Israeli form of showing anguish and despair. They would grate their teeth in a menacing fashion.

Job can be considered the father of the expression. He described his miserable comforters as gnashing their teeth (Job 16:9). However, they probably were not biting him. Jesus used the same idiom several times (Matthew 13:50; 22:13; 25:30).

The members of the Sanhedrin sat like angry animals preparing for the kill. Stephen could not doubt their verdict. He looked up into heaven and saw the glory of God with Jesus standing on His right hand. Stephen told his audience what God had shown him.

It isn't easy for twentieth century Gentile Christians to appreciate this scene. Stephen's vision seemed absolute blasphemy. This was the same group which condemned Jesus Christ. How could He be standing on the right hand of God?

They screamed and grabbed their ears. It was too much for them to listen to. In one wave of humanity they rushed toward Stephen. It is safe to imagine he was not treated gently. Flying fists. feet, knees and spittle were likely missiles. The dam had broken and there was no stopping the flood.

The execution of Stephen was not purely a mob action, nor was it entirely illegal. Capital punishment was within the Sanhedrin pale of power. The audience *did* respond angrily, overwhelmed with hate, but within the context of a trial.

Witnesses were necessary to complete any trial (Leviticus 24:14; Deuteronomy 17:7), and they were available. They took off their outer garments because they were expected to cast the first stones. Afterward, a heap of stones was normally used to bury the victim.

If the stoning of Stephen was carried out as most of the others, he was thrown off a cliff. This often caused considerable injury and sometimes killed the victim. One of the witnesses threw the first stone in the hope of crushing his chest. Then anyone in the crowd was welcome to come forward and throw rocks. It had to be a miserable way to die.

The Jews took no pains to make capital punishment appear pleasant. Neither did the Romans in their use of crucifixion. The purpose of execution was to dissuade the living from breaking the law.

If Stephen was stoned in the traditional method, he obviously survived the fall. His adversaries picked up stones a foot or two wide and hurled them down into the gully. Stephen turned immediately to prayer.

Luke records two most impressive things about Stephen's words, possibly the only words he said. He asked Jesus Christ to receive him—further evidence that the Greek martyr considered Jesus to be God. His second concern was his executioners. Stephen didn't want God to charge them with this sin. No vindictiveness or revenge. He followed the spirit of the dying Christ. The young deacon had more than learned his verses; he had acquired a spirit.

Stephen becomes an excellent billboard for well-wishing. If he could ask forgiveness for those who slaughtered him, it gives us all hope. Certainly we can wish well for the auto mechanic who forgot to tighten our oil pan. We can extend a glad hand to our neighbor with the loud stereo.

Stephen "fell asleep," but violently. Sleep became a well-suited euphemism for death among Christians. Even under these conditions a peaceful acceptance of death is possible.

The most famous convert in the history of Christendom walks to center stage at this point. Saul of Tarsus has been a witness to all these proceedings.

Saul was a native of a Cilician city and possibly heard Stephen speak in the Libertine synagogue. At any rate he gave full approval to this execution. The calm manner in which Stephen faced death and the look on his face had a lasting effect on Saul (Acts 22:20).

There is some possibility Saul furnished an eyewitness account for Luke the historian. In death, Stephen may have furnished a greater springboard for Christianity than he ever dreamed.

Something To Think About

1. Are there prejudices among your local group of Christians? Against ethnic groups? Against the poor or rich? The young or old?
2. Was Stephen wise in his approach to the Libertine synagogue? Did he suffer from a lack of tact? Do some Christians turn you off?
3. Do you have friends who seem particularly peaceful under stress? Does faith play a role?
4. Are Christians humble? Should they be?
5. Is Stephen too blunt in Acts 7:51-52? How do "frank" Christians affect you?
6. What is Stephen's attitude toward his executioners? What does it teach us about wishing well to our enemies?
7. What part do you see Saul playing in this execution?

3
TIMOTHY

He Had a Sensitive, Willing Personality

Young people have a healthy mixture of zest and unpredictability. Their enthusiasm makes your eyes sparkle with amazement. Their surprises keep you on your toes and more than a little anxious.

This is probably the best way to describe Timothy. His dedication and energy bordered on the dazzling. But he also added a dozen gray hairs to Paul's frosty crown.

We aren't certain how Timothy came to know Christ as a personal experience. Paul refers to him as his "child," but this doesn't necessarily mean he introduced him to Christianity. Somewhere he crossed the path of a dedicated disciple and was converted.

Timothy's background included a mixed family. His mother was Jewish and his father was a Greek. Because of unresolved religious differences, his training became a combination of both dedication and neglect. He was raised as a Jew and yet not completely. Consequently the Jews said he was a Greek while the Greeks insisted he was a Jew.

This is why mixed marriages were discouraged among the Jews. The more conservative considered it heretical to wed a non-Jew and were vocal about it. As usual, children suffer from debates among adults. If Timothy was like the others, he had heard more than one slur thrown his way.

Not that Timothy didn't have parents who cared. His mother, Eunice, is one of the few mothers personally commended in the New Testament (II Timothy 1:5). Even his grandmother Lois is recognized for her faithful contribution. A solid mother must have helped a great deal, but life can still be tough in a world of prejudice and intolerance.

The hate between Jews and Samaritans went back over 400 years. At the bottom of their problem was basic prejudice. Samaritans were a mixed race and others couldn't stand it. Even Greeks who had converted to Judaism were distrusted by some racial segments. Hate seems to affect people all over the world.

Timothy came into the Christian life open-faced and excited. He was more like a morning glory than a person: fresh, tender, colorful and eager.

His hometown Christians thought highly of him and said so. Lystra was halfway between Iconium and Derbe. Timothy's reputation was healthy in all three places. Lystra wasn't an easy town for practicing believers, for there a temple to Jupiter served as the center of pagan worship (Acts 14:13), and the reception of preachers was not warm.

Somehow, in the process of being born a half-Jew, Timothy had failed to be circumcised. Under normal circumstances this would be no big problem, and his

Jewish-Greek friends never considered this an issue. But his new life and ambition to serve Christ were presenting some odd difficulties.

Circumcision has been practiced among the Jews since the time of Abraham (Genesis 17:10-14). Later it became a distinction between believers and non. The subject became so hot a debate that Antiochus Epiphanes outlawed the practice. In response, Mattathias forcefully circumcised many Jews.

As more Greeks became Jews, the rite declined among the converts, probably for several reasons. To begin with, the adults could not have been too eager to submit to circumcision. It had to be painful at best and embarrassing at worst. Also, some Greek-Jews refused to circumcise their children.

When Timothy became a Christian, this simple oversight became an issue. Timothy wanted to serve Christ and Paul wanted to take him along on his journeys. But in the areas where they were to visit there were large numbers of Jews. They distrusted Greek-Jews and despised the uncircumcised ones.

We can't sell short the enormous dedication of Timothy. He didn't become half a Christian and wouldn't take his discipleship lightly. He had the freedom to reject circumcision. If others didn't like it, they could sit around and pout. But Timothy decided to forego his Christian liberty.

Only strong people can do that. The weak and insecure have more trouble letting go. Not that we would have faulted Timothy if he had stood up for his rights. He was entitled to them. In fact, Paul most likely would have stood up with the young man if that was the direction he chose. He defended Titus' right to refuse circumcision (Galatians 2:3). After all, circumcision didn't mean anything since Christ had fulfilled the law.

But Timothy saw it as an opportunity to give of himself. Both sides of the issue were clearly worth defending. Liberty was a valid concept and should not be disregarded. Service was also a valuable commodity and was no less important. Timothy decided to select one while Titus took the other. Two good men championing two excellent causes.

Sometimes people must choose between two goods. This sounds like an enviable position, but it is difficult nevertheless. Do we give to the Cancer Foundation, the Kidney Foundation or split the money? Two good options but hard ones all the same.

It is an ethical crisis. If Titus was correct, how can Timothy be? But it only reaches agonizing proportions if we are used to simplistic solutions. The fact is, two people can disagree sharply and both of them be correct. The people who celebrate communion once a quarter may be as right as those who serve it monthly or weekly. The real rub comes when one of the groups believes it is exclusively correct.

Right comes in different colors. Evil does, too. It is right to work, to play tennis, to sleep. Three different people may pick one of these to do at lunch time, and all three are correct. Learning this is the first step to appreciating others who don't agree with us.

Thanks for being circumcised, Timothy. You taught a great deal about flexibility in serving Christ.

Was Titus a lesser Christian for rejecting circumcision? By no means. Timothy could point no self-righteous finger at his brother. Sometimes Christians sacrifice and then belittle those who don't. It is a cheap practice. It is like the person who goes on a diet and then castigates those who don't. Or like the person who swears off desserts and then sits in judgment over those who enjoy them. It is a beggarly attitude. Fortunately, Timothy resisted this spicy temptation.

With the circumcision crisis out of the way, Paul, Silas and Timothy took off "to the sea" (Acts 17:14). All of Asia Minor looked like an open door and their adrenalin was running high.

It didn't take long for Timothy to get into the thick of battle. We find him at Berea with Paul and Silas when the going got tough (Acts 17:13).

Some non-believers traveled all the way from Thessalonica just to harrass the disciples. Soon crowds were stirred up and the trio was clearly in danger. Since Paul was the center of the controversy, the local believers thought he had better leave.

Timothy and Silas remained at Berea and tried to tie the work together until Paul eventually made his way to Athens and sent for his co-workers.

By the time Timothy and Silas caught up with Paul, he had made his way to Corinth. The two devoted friends played an important role at this juncture in the apostle's life.

Things had not gone well for Paul. In several cities he had faced opposition and open hostility. By now he had started making tents to support himself. Fortunately, he met fellow tentmakers Aquila and Priscilla. They were Jews who had been evicted from Rome under Claudius in A.D. 49.

To Paul, Timothy and Silas must have looked as good as a tax refund. It was hard enough being part of an unpopular cause. Loneliness made the job all the more difficult. An expressive people, the three friends didn't stand around like mannequins merely shaking hands. It is easy to see them hugging, back-slapping and rubbing each other on the head. Their smiles probably soon burst into laughter, while their hearts leaped like playful colts.

Friendship is a tonic which no person can match. The disciples were oddly human and definitely need-ed each other. Timothy had traveled many miles to make this reunion a reality.

A few years ago a missionary friend held a meeting 300 miles from my home. When he was finished he sent his family home to Pennsylvania. Charlie caught a plane and came to visit me for four or five days. What a lift! Just to realize he cared enough to go that far out of his way to get in touch. If Timothy helped Paul as much as Charlie helped me, the story is easy for me to appreciate.

Timothy not only brought himself, but his arsenal was packed with two other essentials. First, the youthful Christian brought good news. Things were going well at Thessalonica (I Thessalonians 3:6). The new Christians had a reputation and witness which wouldn't quit. Everyone who traveled in and out of the harbor was gossiping about these changed lives.

Second, the apostle Paul was in need of financial assistance. He had not turned to tent making for ex-ercise. Nor was Paul trying to impress the popula-tion. The truth of the matter was that he was broke. His ability to preach the gospel was seriously handi-capped because he had to find employment.

Timothy and Silas had brought finances from the Christians at Philippi. This also added to Paul's ex-citement and he never forgot their generosity. They were the only ones who were thoughtful during those "down" days for the apostle (Philippians 4:15, II Corinthians 11:8 ff).

It is true that Paul played the important role in opening Corinth to the gospel, but those who carried out supporting roles were just as vital. If the believers at Philippi had not collected money the work would have been considerably harder. If Timothy had been unwilling to carry that offering, Paul would have continued working with leather goods. Timothy became the essential connection. Paul now gave himself exclusively to the preaching of the Word.

The fibers of friendship were drawing tighter between Timothy and Paul. At Corinth, a new depth of will developed. Timothy gained new responsibilities. His personality grew, with its many complexities and strengths.

Every shy Christian in the world should draw encouragement from Timothy. He appears to have had an uncomfortable mixture of drive and bashfulness. Timothy wanted to get into the thick of the battle, and yet he was reticent at the same time. In modern times, his relatives are as plentiful as pigeons in a park.

Paul was going to put Timothy to work, but it was bound to present problems. Somehow Timothy did not carry an aura of confidence and authority. His demeanor didn't do justice to his ability. Timothy's dedication would match anyone's. His knowledge and knack for getting the job done were excellent. But somehow he had trouble convincing people he could control the situation.

A police sergeant told me he had an officer in a

similar situation. The policeman was as short as the regulations would allow. Consequently, many people had trouble taking him seriously. Even writing out a traffic ticket could be a hazardous experience. People would badger, insult, threaten and even fight the youthful officer. Fortunately he could take care of himself. But sometimes it made his job all the challenge he wanted.

Timothy had the tools. Yet there was some question as to whether he could get the message of his ability across. To make matters worse, his assignment at Corinth was a tough territory. It probably resembled a port bar more than a church. The converts were rude and crude. They had gotten drunk at some of the church feasts. A few were living in open sexual sin and the congregation had no heart to take action.

The church probably needed an old-fashioned drill instructor, but they were getting a poet. He had a feel for the people and a terrific compassion, but Timothy was in for a rocky road of tough knocks.

Paul realized the situation at the Corinthian church was deteriorating. He asked the local congregation to give Timothy a chance. He had a great deal to offer. Paul knew the group could be hard on anyone and he asked them to be at peace with Timothy (I Corinthians 16:10-11).

But this church was in no pleasant mood. They were making fists and flexing muscles. Their respect for Paul was boring rapidly into the ground. Timothy could have been a tremendous help (I Corinthians 4:17) but they weren't in the humor for listening.

Finally Timothy left Corinth. We can't be sure of the circumstances surrounding his leaving or of his feelings. Was he disillusioned? Were there bitter words? Whatever the reason, it was better for him to move on. Paul sent Titus to take Timothy's place.

Timothy's hands may have been perfectly clean at Corinth. Perhaps the full gamut of his talents could never be appreciated in that setting. Sometimes good men are turned off by testy congregations. They have contempt for gentleness and only understand dogmatism and absolute authority. The person who is willing to give and take is sometimes swallowed up by an arrogant collection of Christians.

It is hard to evaluate what this experience did to Timothy's confidence. We do know it didn't seem to alter his brisk, loving spirit. He continued his close association with Paul and traveled widely. Timothy visited local churches to inquire about their welfare. He evidently returned to the Philippi area and ministered to the believers at Colossae. Timothy made visits throughout Macedonia.

Eventually Timothy bade farewell to the road and settled down to become the pastor of the church at Ephesus, at least for awhile. The church grew well. The Word was preached and many other communities were affected. They paid a price with opposition from both Jews and pagans, but when they had finished, a formidable church was established.

Even though Timothy was established at Ephesus, Paul's love and concern for him still reached across the miles. The apostle wrote two personal letters to give Timothy advice on how to pastor. They were published in the New Testament as I and II Timothy. A similar letter was written to Titus.

When Paul left Timothy at Ephesus, he was fully aware of the problems which flanked the church.

Many of the local people greatly resented a Christian congregation. Those who were converted often came from pagan backgrounds. Some carried over their superstitions and spilled them into the church. For all of its progress, the alloy of beliefs also created an unhealthy tension.

But what particularly interests us in the Pastoral Epistles is their light on Timothy's personality. We see him as a bashful disciple who pays heavily. Yet despite his persistent handicap, he hung in there. Paul tried to encourage him and help lighten the load. His advice has been used beneficially by Christians for centuries.

The words Paul used to encourage Timothy are first class: They have sparkle, zest and boldness. Paul "charges," "commands" to "fight the good fight"; he "urges" Timothy to "point out" the truth to his congregation. There was nothing indecisive about the Apostle Paul. He wanted his follower in the faith to catch the same spirit.

One of the problems which seemed to bother Timothy was his relative youth. The question of his youth had to be an apparent factor rather than a real one. After all, he was old enough to stay out late! By this time he had been associated with Paul for fifteen years. This probably put him in the 35-40 bracket. The word for youth had been used to describe 40-year-old military officers.

Maybe Timothy looked younger than his actual years (a curse which doesn't afflict most of us). Those who do look youthful sometimes resent it. Some of us grow mustaches or change our clothing to give a seasoned effect. It is embarrassing to meet someone and think she is a sister only to find out she is the mother.

We have to believe Timothy looked young. Some congregations can never adjust to a youthful-looking minister. They are looking for wisdom with just a touch of gray. Consequently they have missed some excellent teachers and counselors.

In all probability, Timothy's lack of confidence made him seem even younger. In an effort to be fair he tried to see all sides. Others interpreted this as indecision. They decided to take advantage of him. They were looking down on this youthful upstart (I Timothy 4:12).

Paul assured Timothy that he had the gifts, and that he shouldn't let anyone bluff him out of it. There was no need to change. He should hang in there and keep doing what was right. Some young people are fools, but others are wise as the ages.

The hardships and pressures were starting to leave their mark on Timothy. As with many others, stress over an extended period was beginning to hurt. He tried shrugging off the insults. On occasion, he fought back. Neither was easy for a peace-loving, sensitive man.

Whatever the exact nature of his infirmities, we know they were intense. Some authorities speculate he was an invalid by now, but it is all too hard to determine. Paul's recommendation that Timothy try a little wine for medicinal purposes (I Timothy 5:23) does demonstrate honest concern for his health. If Timothy's ailments were caused by stress, he certainly had plenty of cause. At one time or another most of the ceiling had fallen on his head.

In some places the pastorate greatly resembles the first century situation at Ephesus. Too many pastors are using buttermilk to keep an ulcer at bay.

One congregation is often split into four or five divisions. Segment A thinks the pastor is an evangelist. Section B sees him as a hand holder and massager. C pictures the same man as a teacher spouting outlines and parsing verbs. Segment D looks for color and exciting sermons aimed at keeping everyone soothed and entertained. E wants an administrator who can organize and keep the machine going. It is no wonder some pastors get burned from all sides.

Fortunately, other congregations are levelheaded and reasonable. They expect their pastor to lead a balanced, satisfying life. This relationship is more enjoyable all the way around.

Timothy was a well-qualified disciple. He was not strong in either evangelism or pastoring. But he was a capable, dedicated, willing heart. Paul saw all of this in him. He mentioned it and commended his outgoing spirit.

Something To Think About

1. Would you consider being re-baptized to join a local church? Does Timothy's example on circumcision help us decide?
2. Can you think of a situation where two people differ greatly and both are right?
3. Is your local church, group, class or family good at befriending others? Why does it work the way it does?
4. Are your Christian leaders lonely? Do members of your group feel free to socialize with them? Would you care if

they had special friends?

5. Are we looking for "super hero" leaders? Is there too much emphasis on the political leader, movie star, football player Christian? Can a shy, knowledgeable Christian find a place in leadership?

6. Do Christian churches and other groups demand too much from their leaders? Are there too many pressures on your present leaders? How can we help improve the situation?

7. In your opinion, why does Timothy need something soothing for his stomach?

4
APOLLOS

Gracious and Capable, He Filled the Gap

I was on my way to talk to a psychologist some 70 miles away. He had read my manuscript on suicide before its final revision. There was no doubt I needed the help he could offer. But I was still ambivalent. How would I hold up when my book was given close criticism? After all, it was my creation and I knew I wouldn't enjoy another personality stamped on it.

This must be a problem which touches all of us. On the surface we recognize the need for help. But underneath, we resent personal criticism.

Certainly Apollos must have suffered from the same conflict. He was busy in the work of the Lord and extremely capable. Confident in his personal life, Apollos wasn't necessarily looking for advice.

The Scriptures tell us several things concerning his background. He was part of the ancient Jewish community living in Alexandria, the capital of Egypt. A large section of the city was allotted for the Hebrew nationality. They had their own governing official, similar to a mayor, who argued the cause of rights of the Jews. The Jewish influence was so great they may have made up one-third of the city. They maintained a large university and library.

Apollos entered the New Testament with this rich cosmopolitan flavor. By some influence he had been introduced to the gospel of the risen Christ. The transition could not have been easy. For practically every Jew, conversion represented major emotional surgery. The higher percentage of his friends had to be shocked and insulted at his new faith.

Christianity spread to Alexandria in a number of ways. Paul and Luke spent much of their time describing its increase between Jerusalem and Rome. However, the actives were also feverish to the south. In years to come Clement, Origen and Pantaenus, as well as the Hellenistic Jew, Philo, all taught in Alexandria. The Good News was spreading rapidly. The martyrdom of Stephen also helped give wings to the mission.

From this setting came a dedicated Christian named Apollos. His assets were impressive. He was an eloquent man, had a brilliant knowledge of the Scriptures and a burning desire to serve. These attributes were locked into more than enough courage.

Not only did he have self-confidence, but he also carried its aura. People could tell he had it all together. No uncertain voice nor dancing eyes. Well versed and capable, Apollos wasn't looking for advice; he was giving it.

The word eloquent (*logios*) literally means logical. Learned, skillful, gifted, there was solid sense to what he said. His iron-tight mind was accompanied by a warm heart. He had a passion for what he did and not merely an intellect.

This collection of high qualities shows he was on the ball. His goals were well determined and his mission settled. He wasn't the type who was looking for criticism or was likely to sit still for it.

Apollos had been taught in "the way of the Lord." There is reason to believe this became the colloquial name for Christians. They were the people of "The Way." Originally, the phrase appears in the Old Testament (Psalm 1:6), but Jesus gave it new meaning. Christ referred to Himself as "The Way" (John 14:6). Apparently both the early believers and their detractors picked up on the term.

Luke tells us Felix was well acquainted with The Way (Acts 24:22). Paul told Felix, "But this I confess unto thee, that after the way which they call heresy, so worship I the God of my fathers . . ." (Acts 24:14, cf. 19:9).

We can only guess how the term is used when it applies to Apollos. But it is interesting to see it used twice in reference to the Egyptian (Acts 18:25, 26). Possibly the title was already growing in popularity.

Despite his excellent credentials, Apollos was doing something incorrectly. Probably not an earth-shaking error—just enough to irritate his audiences. But then, some small pieces of sand can knock out an entire machine.

We have to assume the problem was minor because the author downplays it. After announcing his excellent credentials, Luke summarizes them by saying that he spoke with great fervor and taught about Jesus accurately (verse 25). How many people receive the flamboyant accolades laid on Apollos? He taught the truth of Jesus Christ correctly. Certainly a high compliment.

But people were touchy just as they often are today. They may look for their pet theme or favorite wrinkle in a sermon. If it is missing, some audiences are rattled immediately. One group is so heavy on prophecy they gauge all good preaching by that standard. Any deviation from their accepted outline and their teeth start to gnash.

Probably all of us suffer from some sort of shibboleth (Judges 12:6). When someone says it our favorite way, our eyes shine like gold. When it is mispronounced, we shrink faster than a paycheck.

Apollos' itinerary brought him to Ephesus, a large seaport in Asia. We aren't certain how Christianity was first introduced to the area; possibly Jewish pilgrims brought it back from Jerusalem.

Because of his Jewish background the main interest of Apollos was the local synagogue. They were still open to Christian speakers, though hostilities were starting to fester. Many converts were gathered from these meetings. Christianity was considered by most as a Jewish movement with a Hebrew constituency. Paul may have spoken in this same synagogue (Acts 18:19).

In the audience, two people were listening who were to have a dramatic effect on Apollos' life. Priscilla and Aquila decided to stick their necks out and invest themselves in someone's life. Always a risky business, it can be rewarding.

A Mennonite church in Kansas invited a special youth speaker to address their congregation one evening. An interesting person, he had some particularly challenging things to say. However, some of his mannerisms were irritating. Even his plea for dedication was presented in such a way it offended a number of people.

One man in the church decided he would take a chance. He moved directly after the service to invite the speaker to join his family for coffee. The young man accepted with typical enthusiasm.

During the relaxed hour the church member was bold enough to make a couple of suggestions. He told his guest, "You could have an excellent ministry among the Mennonites. We really need what you have to say." Then he kindly explained the two things which were irritating.

Why get involved? They would probably never meet again, but this gentleman wanted to help. Would the lad feel insulted? Would he ignore the advice? This man felt it was worth the risk, and he genuinely helped a young minister.

Priscilla and Aquila decided to launch the same venture. Apollos was doing well. Why should he listen to them? But this couple stuck their necks out.

Aquila was a Hebrew living in Pontus, Italy. Claudius had ordered all Jews expelled from the country, so he and his wife Priscilla had left. We don't know where they became Christians, but the two met Paul at Corinth. They were tentmakers and so shared their trade with the apostle.

When Paul left Corinth he took Aquila and Priscilla with him to Ephesus. Paul moved on to Rome but the husband and wife team remained to work in evangelism. They frequented a synagogue and there heard Apollos.

Now they had to decide whether to get involved. Would they risk rebuff to help Apollos? It would take energy and a little daring. They voted yes.

This particular situation was potentially explosive for at least two reasons. One problem was exercising enough tact to gain his confidence. The second was the question of a woman giving advice to an established Christian. Either one could lead to a headache.

The problem of tact was handled smoothly. Rather than raise an objection in public, they calmly and politely invited Apollos to their home. Anyone who has seen harsh words exchanged in a church foyer can appreciate this move. There was no way to tell how the Egyptian would take this intrusion. If he was cocky and insulted, the scene could have been ugly.

It is easy to bark a few remarks passing in a foyer. They are filled with emotion but little understanding or compassion—criticism without the heart to help. Presenting such proposals privately is often the difference between heat and light.

Many concerned persons could help their pastor if they would learn to do so gently. First they must go to him with kindness and a good sense of humor. Often ministers are greatly improved by a loving, patient member.

The second difficulty was the presence of a woman correcting a man. In most cultures it would be hard to receive, and the Hebrews were no exception.

It is possibly significant that Luke lists Priscilla before her husband. In some cases this means nothing, but here it may have importance. Mrs. Aquila was probably taking the lead in the discussion. This isn't to say she always did. But on this occasion she seemed to be the more aggressive—possibly she was also the more charming.

There is no need to see women in leadership as

brash and bossy. They also can be intelligent, decisive and helpful. Many situations could be helped by heeding the good counsel of women. Possibly many husbands could avoid considerable agony if they would listen to their wives more often.

Fortunately, Priscilla wasn't too inhibited to help. On the other side, Aquila wasn't too insecure to allow her to help. Priscilla had something to contribute and her husband wasn't going to harpoon her. Maybe this is why Paul speaks of them so often (Romans 16:3; I Corinthians 16:19; II Timothy 4:19).

Priscilla and Aquila seemed mature enough to handle the subject. The question now was Apollos. How would he field criticism under these circumstances? The answer is short in coming. Their advice probably didn't take long, and the issue was solved. No sign of belligerent arguing or touchiness.

After the intimate discussion, the author doesn't tell us Apollos was re-baptized. In fact, he completely ignores the alterations. Does Luke do this because the change was of little duration? Would it seem silly to us or possibly escape us altogether? After all, what was an urgent issue then may mean nothing to us today. Luke doesn't consider it worth mentioning.

Whatever the situation, all three emerge as giants. They grew together—Apollos was not insistent on having his own way, and Aquila and Priscilla were not determined to push their weight around.

Apollos instantly became acceptable to the local believers. The stamp of approval landed and everyone was offering encouragement. How could they help? What was the next step? What ministry did Apollos have in mind?

It was a fresh new picture—so different from

thousands of other disagreements which end in bitterness.

Apollos felt he should leave for Achaia. Over there he would move to its leading city of Corinth. The traveling evangelist was destined to play an important role in this area.

The Christians at Ephesus were so pleased with their new friend that they wrote letters of introduction. This was a common practice, since strangers could claim anything. A cordial epistle would be terribly helpful in breaking the ice.

At Corinth he became friends with the Christians and evangelized Jews. He must have been an encouragement to the collection of believers there. Any capable assistance was welcome.

Paul had been to Corinth and had preached in the synagogue. For a year and a half the apostle shared in the Christian community—consequently, there were few strangers to the "Way" when Apollos set out.

The Egyptian was destined to make a considerable mark on Corinth. He debated the Jews in head-on, public clashes. These debates were common and caused many to make up their minds both ways (see chapters on Stephen and Paul), and often they were conducted in the face of enormous hostility.

Apollos' approach was a heavily scriptural presentation. The early Christians believed they could prove the Messiahship of Jesus from the Old Testament, since He had fulfilled large numbers of verses with exactness. When confronted with the evidence, many Jews were persuaded, but others were not.

In public debate, Apollos had to be an impressive figure. He was intelligent, powerful and convincing.

His delivery could be paralyzing to his opponents.

Certainly, some rulers of the synagogues were well-trained in the Scriptures. Others, however, had allowed it to slide. They spent so much time arguing over the traditions of the fathers that the Scriptures had become foreign territory (Mark 7:8-12). They made simple mistakes born of elementary ignorance of the Old Testament.

When the rabbis looked bad publicly, the results were predictable. Part of the crowd sided with the beleagured leaders; others were attracted to the cool Biblical logic offered by the Jewish Christians.

Apollos had a distinct ministry in Corinth. Paul had preceded him and done the pioneer work. This didn't mean everyone in the city had heard about the risen Christ, but several groups had. Converts had been made and a nucleus of Christians had been established—Paul had planted the seed; now Apollos was watering the garden.

Luke paints a portrait of Apollos as the apex of graciousness. Capable but not insulting. A man of conviction but politely adjustable. He is a distant cry from some famous Christian leaders. Apollos is not the harried Christian executive heading a "ministry" corporation. He doesn't appear to be concerned over who gets the credit.

Our society is filled with people who overestimate their own importance. They think the thing they do is the most significant in all the world. Such Christian leaders are terrible bores. They fail to see themselves as part of a picture; they come to see themselves as *the* picture.

Some of the mail pleas for money show how acute the problem is. Others demand time in a local pulpit.

Can't we see how crucial their cause is? Can't *they* see what small pieces to the giant puzzle they really contribute?

Apollos was flexible, learning, and modest. He wanted to fill the gap where he was. He was happy with no more and no less.

Other people wanted to turn the Egyptian's head, but he resisted it. During his extensive ministry at Corinth, he collected a large following of converts. Some became confused. They were attracted to Jesus Christ but they also had a strong preference for Apollos. Christians began to divide into camps. Those who followed Apollos became proud and sectarian (I Corinthians 3:4-7).

Under normal conditions, Corinth represented an odd assortment of Christians. There were serious rifts among the believers because of economic differences. The wealthy were not kind to the poor and the poor had little tolerance for the privileged. Some were gluttons and became drunk at the church festivals. Someone has described the situation as more of a gospel mission than a church.

In the congregation's background was a mixture of Judaism and paganism. When they tried to blend, they repelled each other. They began to polarize over their differences. Soon there were separate parties rather than unity in the body of Jesus Christ. One group would raise its proud head and say, "We are of the Paul Party." They were certainly glad they didn't make the serious mistakes the other Christians made.

Another group replied, "But we are of the Apollos Party." They would strut while kneeling in prayer. Their emphases, and in some cases their origins, were different. Each group was competitive and proud. The divisions into sects were natural but dastardly.

As this attitude grew, Apollos was called on again to show his true mettle. A collection of Christians wanted to treat him as their special guru. He would be their party leader.

The offer was tempting. It gave him a "name" and a dose of prestige — hard for any aspiring minister to resist. But he did. When Paul wrote of the warring parties in Corinth he made no criticism of the Egyptian missionary. Like himself, Apollos had made no attempt to prompt this spirit. He had no thirst for power or acclaim. He was a dedicated servant of Christ and happy to be one.

Something To Think About

1. Why is criticism so hard to handle?
2. Make some suggestions on how to correct a Christian brother.
3. Can you name some "shibboleths" that your Christian group looks for?
4. Can you name a time when you have accepted criticism to your benefit?
5. Would it bother you to be corrected by a woman? Explain.
6. Do you feel Christian pleas for money are overdone?
7. Are Christian divisions healthy or harmful?

5
PETER

He Was a "Rock" Slow in Forming

Why would Jesus Christ select a volcano to paint into His scenery on this earth? No doubt He had His reasons. We have no doubt also that He knew the personalities He chose for His disciples. It would have been just as easy for Him to collect a dozen tranquil junior executives. Instead, He called together a wide assortment of fireworks.

If we consider the disciples as fireworks, Peter wasn't a sparkler. No quiet light for him. Simon was like a rocket with a faulty fuse. There was no way of knowing when or if he would go off.

Whatever problems Peter faced as a disciple, he shines like new armor in the book of Acts. During the first twelve chapters he is indisputably the leading character in the Christian church. The midwife at its birth, Peter is responsible for Christianity's safe delivery, a healthy smack and warm clothing. It arrived with robust cheeks and a reassuring cry. The fisherman saw to it.

Jesus didn't make the mistake many of us would have made. Often we are drawn to pleasant, secure, even predictable personalities. They are the safest. Christ saw potential beyond the facade. If Peter was noisy, it didn't rattle the Messiah. When Peter was impetuous, Jesus was patient. Even when Simon was cowardly, Christ could easily see beyond that. Peter would make it. All he needed was time and understanding.

It is interesting to see how greatly he improved after the resurrection. Yet, Peter never did smooth away all the rough edges entirely. Peter and Paul, two giant men of God, stood toe to toe and mixed harsh words. But then, none of the apostles even approached perfection.

Peter's personality speaks out loudly against many modern cries for conformity. Many Christian organizations seem to think their strength lies in everyone buckling under. They want everyone to think alike, live similar lifestyles and gleefully accept each program. Groups love to go to work on a Christian's personality — we know he is "spiritual" when he "conforms." Fortunately, Jesus could see much deeper.

Modern Christians should have worked with the disciples! The golden dozen resembled Silly Putty more than a mold.

Peter was woven tightly into Christianity. He had experienced almost every part of it. His best friends and business partners, James and John, were early followers of Christ. Simon's brother, Andrew, was one of the first believers.

Of all the crowds and disciples, Christ had three particular friends. His needs for a few truly close friends were much like ours. The intimate trio were Peter, James and John.

If the life of Christ had a profound effect on Peter the fisherman, the resurrection was explosive. No longer the vacillating fickle follower, Simon's determination after Christ's resurrection became immovable. He clearly became a transformed man when the risen Christ ascended into heaven. He gave suggestions, preached sermons and stood jaw to jaw with opposing officials.

After the resurrection, the first major decision the Christians had to face as a group was a replacement for Judas. Simon took the leadership and suggested the 120 select a twelfth disciple. Quickly and efficiently, Matthias was chosen and the Christians were rolling (Acts 1:15 ff). Jesus called Peter "the Rock" because He knew what the fisherman was really made of.

Peter's potential began to surface graphically at Pentecost. It had been fifty days since Christ had been crucified and now the Spirit started to move with special force (Acts 2). Jews had gathered from the wide corners of the earth to celebrate Pentecost. It was an ideal time to explain the good news of Jesus Christ.

At this gathering, Peter became the principal speaker and defender of the faith. The Christians weren't drunk as some thought. They were filled with the power of the Holy Spirit. Peter explained to the skeptics where that power had come from. Before he was finished, Simon described the fantastic miracle God had done in sending Jesus Christ to earth. Now it was possible to be free from the guilt of sin by believing in the Messiah. Jesus was God's anointed one.

The response was enormous. Three thousand immediately volunteered to be baptized. The forgiveness of Jesus Christ was the best news they had ever heard. Baptism was the appropriate response for those who believed.

Without hesitation, the apostles and their fellow Christians began a training program — a discipleship course (Acts 2:42-47). Their fellowship was strong and their sharing was generous. They were not yet pouring their money into buildings and programs. Their first concern was to provide for each other so no one would suffer. Many gave up everything they owned. Others gathered supplies for famine-stricken areas. The pattern was established with the first few thousand converts (Acts 4:32-37), and in some places it still continues though there are millions of believers.

No one doubted that these post-resurrection Christians were as earnest as when Christ walked among them. When Peter and John healed a lame man at the Gate Beautiful (Acts 3:2), everyone knew that Christianity was still alive and well. Peter used the occasion to preach the gospel.

The priests and Sadducees were immediately vexed. They had worked hard to stamp out this Christian menace, and were counting on the crucifixion to stop this Messiah nonsense. But now it was raging like a forest fire in August.

Peter and John were arrested and brought before the Sanhedrin. This was a different fisherman than the one they had met a short time before at Jesus' arrest (Matthew 26:69 ff). No wavering or cowardice this time. He stood boldly in front of his old enemies, the high priests Annas and Caiaphas. But this time he was telling them that Jesus Christ, whom the priests had executed, was alive. God had raised Him from the dead (Acts 4:5-12).

There are few things as powerful in the propagation of the gospel as changed lives. A teenage girl was telling about her wrestles with her faith in Jesus Christ. Sometimes her faith was strong and vital. At other times it resembled a wagon with a broken axle. But there was one thing she was sure of—her parents were completely new people. Since Christ had met them, they had become almost totally transformed. This living fact always helped when she was down.

Peter's judges marveled at what they saw and heard. The council finally decided to let the pair go; however, they stipulated that they could no longer teach in the name of Jesus. The priests underestimated the fisherman. He was no longer the man who had been intimidated by a young maiden (Matthew 26:69). Peter had no intention of quitting teaching and told them so.

The Sanhedrin threatened Peter and John again, but these Christians were past being intimidated. They had settled their accounts with God and weren't about to be bullied out of their faith.

The council was now more than a little afraid of the growing crowds. They were a swelling group which now exceeded 5,000 (Acts 4:4). The day of dealing with a motley dozen or a disorganized 120 was over. Now the Sanhedrin had better be careful what they did.

Peter went directly back to the job of preaching. Their winds were strong and they had every intention of keeping their sails high.

The infant church was filled with enthusiasm and sacrifice, but at the same time it had internal problems. One of the first serious ones involved money, and Peter launched right into the middle of it. As we know, many voluntarily sold their personal goods and gave the proceeds to the apostles, although they were in no way forced to do so.

Ananias and Sapphira were a Christian couple who agreed to sell their belongings and donate the proceeds to the apostle's relief fund. They were anxious to please their new friends, but unfortunately the pair allowed their eagerness to overrule their good sense. They may have had some good intentions. They desperately wanted to be accepted. In all fairness to them, they may have wanted also to give away part of their goods to help others. But somewhere motives became mixed, and they decided to scheme.

The couple sold a piece of land the same way many other Christians had, but they were torn between keeping some of the proceeds and giving it all to the church. How could they be accepted as first-rate Christians and still keep part of the money? they wondered. There was only one way. There was no need to give it all. They would merely make it look like they did.

Does this sound crooked and deceitful? To be sure. But it is also understandable. Ananias and Sapphira would make good patron saints for many of us. We have all done ridiculous things to impress each other. Too often after we become Christians we continue to play the same games. We carry our insecurities into the church.

Some of us attend Christian concerts which we

couldn't begin to appreciate. Others give testimonies because Jane and Joe Doe are doing it. Still others agree to peculiar doctrines which they don't actually believe. All bowing down to the pressure to impress each other. The more we change, the more we are the same.

Somehow Peter knew immediately what had happened. In his mind there could be no compromise here. The church could not be allowed to start on deceitful premises like this.

Peter confronted Ananias and made sure everyone understood the situation. No one had to give his property (Acts 5:4)—it was theirs to keep or give. But it was *not* theirs to deceive. They had tried to lie to their fellowman. In fact, they had lied to God.

When Ananias heard this harsh condemnation he immediately fell dead. Was it caused by natural or supernatural causes? None of us can say with certainty. The young men who watched took his body and buried it quickly.

Possibly the whole scene sounds cruel and unloving, but for Peter the matter was crucial. He couldn't allow the emerging church to grow in corruption. If he did, it would be on a par with the pagan religions around them.

If Peter's attitude had persisted through the centuries, the church would have been far better off. Some Christian business dealings have been more than shady. More than one letter has misrepresented the financial conditions of a Christian organization.

A Christian magazine reported a special plea by a missionary organization. Their headquarters had burned down and they were raising a large sum to replace the building. The reporter said the letter failed to mention that the structure was fully insured.

Possibly some of us are more concerned with image than honesty. Fortunately, most individuals and organizations are extremely careful; however, there is enough shoddy practice to concern all of us.

When we read through Acts, two problems keep recurring in the early church. One is equality; there is much debate over the admission of Gentiles. The second is money (widows' fund, Simon Magus, famine relief). These were the rough edges being hammered out on the anvil of immaturity.

Following the progress that the church made may be good guidelines for the modern church. In some places both of these problems are handled excellently. Other groups have even worse problems in these areas than the first century church.

Peter could not take the deception issue lightly, but it would be difficult for us to hold the apostle culpable in Ananias' death. Three hours later the fisherman interrogated Sapphira with equal firmness. She repeated the previous lie. Peter told her bluntly what had happened to her husband.

When Sapphira heard of her husband's death, she collapsed at the feet of Peter. In a second, she too was dead. The same men who had buried her husband carried her out also (Acts 5:10).

A question as to Ananias' and Sapphira's true Christianity has to arise. It is a fair question, even if it is impossible to answer. What they did was clearly not Christian. Peter made a dramatic point of this. However, behavior cannot be the total criteria for judging belief. I have done a number of things which I would not consider Christian. Pardon me, but I am suspicious you have, too.

Can a non-believer lie to the Holy Spirit? There is not enough evidence here to prove they were not Christian. Only enough to demonstrate enormous immaturity. We are members of a large club.

The real message of the story is found in Acts 5:11. Tremendous fear spread through the church. The basic message of the gospel is peace and release from fear; yet, some fear is healthy. The absence of all fear would be dangerous. "Them that sin rebuke before all, that others also may fear" (I Timothy 5:20).

Peter continued with an amazing ministry. He didn't have a public relations assistant or a press agent—he didn't need one. The news of the power of Christ was spreading naturally. People were literally carried for miles just so they could get near the apostle. This healing ministry served as irrefutable proof of the miraculous energy of the gospel.

The high priests became so rattled by the publicity that they had the apostle arrested again. They were indelicate enough to remind Peter that they had forbidden him to preach Christ. Peter in turn reminded them of his primary obligation to obey God (5:29). When the council heard his belligerent reply they decided Peter needed emergency surgery to have his life removed.

Gamaliel, the doctor of law and a Pharisee, intervened and saved the day (Acts 5:34). The respected sage carried considerable weight. He was remembered with great reverence among the Jews. The Mishna claims Israel knew no rabbi like him. One of his more famous pupils was another Pharisee named Saul of Tarsus (Acts 22:3).

Gamaliel persuaded the Sanhedrin to back off from

the Christians. In a form of compromise, they beat the Christians and let them go. It is almost nonchalant to read of the beating of the disciples. I feel no pain as I read about it in my air-conditioned office. There is little to gain by dwelling on the pain; even the apostles didn't brood. They departed "rejoicing" (Acts 5:41). Nevertheless, it was a wrenching experience. Their backs were often ripped open, and the healing was slow.

These beatings were frequent in the early church (Acts 16:22; 16:37; 18:17; 21:32; 22:19). In some countries they may be frequent yet today.

The apostles almost had a footrace back to the temple. They again began to preach the gospel they were told to muzzle. Peter's ministry continued undiminished.

One of Peter's more famous miracles was that of raising Dorcas from the dead (Acts 9:36). No convert presented more repercussions for Peter than did Cornelius (Acts 10, 11). Peter wasn't sure God wanted to save Gentiles, so the conversion of the Gentile centurion was a milestone in Peter's spiritual growth. It proved that even Rocks could be moved.

Not only did Peter baptize Cornelius, but he traveled to Jerusalem to defend his actions. Peter's speech before the Council was monumental in developing an open attitude toward Gentile converts (Acts 15).

Sometimes we picture Peter as a poorly coordinated cluck. It is our loss. Those who knew the man loved him enormously. He needed this personal affection since he received enough hostility from the opposition. On one of his frequent trips to jail, his friends at Jerusalem prayed relentlessly for the man's release (Acts 12:5 ff), and God miraculously freed him.

In this jailhouse incident, Peter was sleeping so soundly the bright light of the angel didn't even wake him. The angel had to hit him in the side. Peter was sleeping peacefully even though Herod might have him executed.

The fisherman remained strong throughout his life and furnished excellent leadership. He wrote two instructive epistles. In the second one he demonstrated a passionate belief in the return of Christ.

Peter, far from a flighty Christian, suffered great pangs of conscience. Throughout his life he continually reflected on the problem of Gentile converts. The apostle defended their full rights before the Council at Jerusalem (Acts 15). But at other times he suffered second thoughts.

The smiling faces of Gentile Christians made them easy to accept. Certainly the vision he received from God was compelling (Acts 10). Yet, his gnawing scruples kept eating away.

Somewhere along Peter's ministry, he and Paul locked horns over the issue. The fisherman had regressed and was now rejecting full acceptance of Gentiles. Paul tells us he confronted Peter face to face over the problem (Galatians 2:11-14).

Often we expect too much out of leaders. We forget their emotions and difficulties. Peter was concrete. But sometimes the ground shifted. He was a lot like us.

Peter traveled a great deal and often took his wife on the trips (I Corinthians 9:5). Tradition says he died as a martyr for the faith.

Something To Think About

1. Are Christians "cliquish" in their selection of personalities? Do we shy away from people who are not like us?

2. Would the church suffer by encouraging more individuality? Is there too much pressure to conform? Not enough? Explain.

3. What was the attitude of the first Christians toward possessions? Do we share our goods with each other? Should we?

4. Do you notice some deception in the handling of Christian finances? If so, what can be done about it?

5. Why is money so often an issue in the Bible?

6. What is the best way to advertise your church or group? How did Peter do it?

7. Are Christians ready to change their minds when they are wrong? What is your experience?

6
PHILIP

He Was Financially Responsible

Could the infant church of Christ survive financial corruption? The early Christians faced no more serious question than this one. It is the exact puzzle which often faces the church today. How much has money damaged the testimony of Jesus Christ? Philip, the evangelist, wades briskly into this problem and helps make some clear-cut guidelines.

Whenever money is handled, there is the prospect of corruption. In the first century the sound of silver often turned the heads of religious leaders. The Roman world saw the bribing of religious officials as a normal, accepted practice. Judaism, with its high standards and reputation, was not untainted (I Samuel 8:3). Even Christianity had faced several scandals during its embryonic existence. We remember Ananias and Sapphira from the previous chapter. Since the church would be made up of human beings, financial trouble was certain.

Philip was a capable, Spirit-filled Christian who

was well spoken of in the community. This dedicated Hellenistic believer was appointed as a deacon at the same time as Stephen and the total seven. (This Philip is not to be confused with the apostle from the Gospel accounts.)

When Stephen was stoned to death, the persecution of the church became white-hot. The pressure was so intense that Christians were forced to flee Jerusalem.

Saul was leading the hunt for Christians. It would be hard to overestimate the role he was playing. He accomplished what the Sanhedrin with all its power could not do. Saul chased the believers out of the security of Jerusalem.

The arch-persecutor was not above dragging men and women out of their homes, imprisoning and even murdering them. Saul went about his job like an eagle after a rodent.

Fear filled the Christians. Consequently, thousands of them spread out into the provinces of Judea and Samaria. Instead of only one city receiving the good news, it would now be spread over an eighty mile area.

Despite all our elaborate plans to share the gospel, much of it has been accomplished by migrations. A nation captures prisoners from another country. These new slaves bring Christianity with them. People are expelled from their land (like the Mennonites) and take the story of Jesus Christ with them. Armies go into other countries and their soldiers and chaplains share the Messiah. It is difficult to know which events God caused and which ones He merely used. But then, maybe it isn't that important to know. The more important point is how such situations are used to good advantage.

Once the Christians started moving from Jerusalem, they found life easier. Eventually, they also invaded the Greek states (Acts 11:19).

Philip soon found himself settled into a city in Samaria. This was an ideal area to preach the gospel. The population consisted of half-breeds who were despised by the Jews. They in turn lost little sleep worrying about their southern neighbors. By preaching here, Philip showed the wide compassion of the gospel.

What a spectacular event! Some ministries are quiet and subtle. Others are strictly the Fourth of July. Philip's visit was cherry bombs and sparklers. The city was entrenched with demon-possessed people. Luke, the author, is specific about their existence but frankly we know little about them. What type of person was possessable? Was it a total thing or something that came and went? Were some of them misdiagnosed cases of epilepsy? Probably all of the above.

There was a large array of people who were subjected to strange phenomena, some of it Satanic. Some of it was national; most of it was misunderstood. There are a number of interesting comparisons with today. People do strange things, hard-to-identify things.

One thing we do know—Philip had a serious impact on the community. Many who previously had "unclean" (Acts 8:7) spirits had them exorcised. People who had spoken in uncontrollable voices no longer had them. Those who at one time had thrown themselves into the fire were now stable. It was no insignificant miracle. People who were lame were now dancing in the streets. Others who had twisted, aching bodies stood tall as pines.

I live in a small town which may be a little larger than the one Philip visited (we are around 4,000). What if a man came to our town and healed everyone? My friend would get rid of his cane, the white-haired lady would lose her limp. The deaf child could throw away his aid. I tried to imagine the impact on our community. The person who did these miracles would gain a following in a minute. Now it is easy to see why there was much "joy" in that city (Acts 8:8).

Philip received a warm reception. The people opened their arms to this amazing man. They also listened intently to his message. It made a great deal of sense. Philip had found fertile soil and was reaping rich rewards for Jesus Christ.

Despite all of this obvious spiritual prosperity, one person only half comprehended the gospel message. Simon was a man well worth knowing. He would have been a fascinating character under any circumstances but he added an odd dimension to Philip's life.

The people of this Samaritan city had tremendous respect for Simon. They considered him a good man, with the power of God. He was a sorcerer with considerable ability. A sorcerer held a unique position in a first century town. Probably the nearest comparison in the English language is witch. Not the black-hatted, stringy-haired broom rider we are used to imagining, but a sorcerer's abilities ran along the same lines.

We aren't certain what wonders he could perform, but they were evidently impressive. He could possibly conjure up voices and sounds and perform healings of some sort. Whatever the procedure, he had gained considerable respect, and the town paid homage to him.

Christians were less receptive to these practitioners. They are called deceitful, immoral; and are placed in the same category as liars and murderers (Galatians 5:19-21; II Timothy 3:8)

Philip's preaching was not only effective with the masses but it also took its toll on Simon the sorcerer. Others were agreeing to be baptized in the name of Jesus Christ—they believed He was the Messiah who forgave sins. The line stretched long with willing converts. Simon was moved by what he heard and saw. He also found it easy to believe and asked to be baptized. When the writer describes Simon's faith there is no reservation, no warning footnote, but later there is reason to question his sincerity. However, at this point, his faith seems to be accepted at face value.

In hindsight, there are some worthwhile lessons to ponder about miracles. In the New Testament they were used as valid apologetics. Not only did Jesus and His disciples use them, but they are sprinkled liberally through the Old Testament. But we cannot deny that Christ had a genuine fear of miracles as a means of conversion.

Many of the miracles performed by Jesus Christ were for compassion's sake and not for conversion. He was moved. Pain, disfigurement, and death definitely bothered Him. Jesus fed multitudes because they were hungry.

He considered miracles a good introduction to the gospel but was leery of them. On at least one occasion many people wanted to believe in Him because of His miracles, and He withdrew Himself (John 2:23 ff). When the Pharisees pushed Christ for a sign, He revolted. Jesus declared that an evil and adulterous generation asks for a sign (Matthew 12:39).

Philip preached Jesus Christ and His kingdom (Acts 8:12), so any lack of sincerity on Simon's part may rest in what Simon *heard*. He may have been so transfixed by the miracles that he heard little of the message. Or it is possible that he believed in the power of Christ. He could have accepted the Messiah on this basis alone—faith without commitment.

We are in the thorny position of trying to judge someone else's faith. What does a person believe? How deeply? How sincerely? We usually end up clumsy and deficient in attempting to measure someone else. As usual, we will have to be content to leave judging to God.

Peter and John had remained at Jerusalem during the hottest days of the persecution. We don't know what life was like; but we are certain personal risks were high. When they received the news of the conversions in Samaria, plans were made to journey north. When they reached Samaria they laid hands on the new converts and each received the Holy Spirit.

Frankly, we are not sure how the Spirit manifested Himself. Did the recipients speak in tongues as they had at Pentecost? It is entirely likely. Were there other indications? That is possible also. We can be reasonably sure the evidence was highly visible. Simon saw something powerful and he wanted it. His mind traveled quickly and naturally to his former life. There was one logical and practical way to receive this gift. Simon would buy it.

Did Simon receive the evidence of the Holy Spirit? Is it possible that he received the power, and then offered to buy the franchise so he in turn could retail it to others? Practically anything is possible. The author does not say Simon was excluded from receiving the Spirit. He never refers to him as a non-believer.

When Simon made the offer to purchase the power, he niched a place for himself in history. Thereafter, whenever a clergyman would try to buy a higher office, his attempt was called "simony." At one time it was a fairly frequent practice. If an individual wanted to become a bishop, he might offer to purchase the office. Often he got it.

But Peter responded to the offer with a sword-like tongue. He was enraged at the suggestion. The apostle told Simon he hoped his money would perish with him. He insisted the sorcerer was not truly converted and should repent immediately (Acts 8:22).

To Peter, Simon the Sorcerer was a "gall of bitterness" (Acts 8:23) and in the bonds of iniquity. Peter's judgment was fast and pointed. There could be no room for Simon's plan. No one could be allowed to even imagine it would or could be tolerated.

Simon was startled at the response. After all, it was only a simple deal. It was no different from any offer he would have made to any other spiritist or magician.

The issue involved is more important than the man Simon. He is difficult to fathom, but the principle isn't. Simon may have been a new Christian and merely resorted to what he knew best. Maybe he didn't realize the full scope of the Christian morality.

Certainly many believers are still using their old set of ethics. Some don't feel their Christian faith has anything to do with personal choices.

But the principle prevails: God is not impressed with money. If we trace Christ's teachings on the subject, we discover He has a near contempt for wealth. He would never consider giving favors or prestige to the financially able.

It is obvious that the problem of giving favors to the wealthy plagued the early church. James spoke vigorously against it (James 2:1-4).

Philip played an important role in this historic moment. He introduced the gospel to Simon. We find the ready evangelist also involved in setting the church straight from the first day.

The time had come to spread the gospel throughout Samaria. On their trip back to Jerusalem, Peter, John and Philip made stops to share the good news. When Philip arrived in Jerusalem, he received a definite visit from the Angel of the Lord (Acts 8:26). God wanted Philip to leave the large city and travel to the desert of Gaza.

A famous road ran southwest of Jerusalem toward Egypt. It was carved through the plains of Philistia and followed near the Mediterranean Sea. In modern times the territory between Gaza and Egypt has been called the Gaza Strip. It is an important route to Israel, Egypt and other nations.

Philip doesn't seem to question the strategy of leaving the teeming city and heading for one sparsely populated. After all, God's plans have always been beneficial though often surprising. This didn't seem the time to begin questioning them. Besides, Jerusalem may still have been an uncomfortable place for a Christian deacon to reside.

En route toward Gaza, Philip found an Ethiopian eunuch sitting in his chariot. This servant of Candace, queen of the Ethiopians, is one of the most interesting characters in the Bible. Strictly speaking, he did not come from the area we presently call Ethiopia. The reference is probably to Nubia further north, running from the Nile at Aswan south to Khartoum.

The Ethiopian held a prominent position in the palace. He was the keeper of the treasury for the queen. Her name was not Candace, but rather her dynasty, so there would be several queens by this name over the generations.

When we think of his chariot, we do a disservice to picture a crude looking western buckboard. In all likelihood it was an elaborately covered wagon with all the splendor of prestige.

Eunuchs, in the service of a queen or the king's harem, usually were castrated so they would be no sexual threat to the women. At other times, however, "eunuch" was a title of office. The men then held the position but were not changed physically.

This man had become a God-fearing Gentile. He became a believer in the God of Israel but not an official Jew. Possibly his status as a eunuch prevented him from being accepted as a Jew. The Jews had strict rules against receiving eunuchs as part of their congregation (Deuteronomy 23:1). However, the time was predicted when such restrictions would be lifted (Isaiah 56:3 ff).

The nameless eunuch was reading the book of Isaiah as he sat by the side of the road. Maybe part of his fascination was chapter 56. When Philip found him, his amazement was fixed on Isaiah 53.

Philip ran toward him. The evangelist had a sense of mission coupled with enthusiasm. It is interesting to see how we run toward some situations and away from others. Our enthusiasm tells us something about our compassion.

Philip looked at the scroll and asked the eunuch if he understood what he was reading. The Ethiopian was completely puzzled. The passage spoke of someone who would be slaughtered. Yet this person would remain humble and speak not a word (Isaiah 53:7).

This was the moment Philip was now living for. From that Old Testament passage the deacon told the eunuch about Jesus Christ.

We aren't privy to everything they discussed. Possibly Philip outlined everything which had happened since the crucifixion. He may have described the resurrection, Pentecost, even the persecution. At any rate he lifted Christ up and let the Ethiopian see Him clearly. In the process, he must have mentioned the thousands who were eagerly baptized in the Messiah's name.

They rode in the chariot as they spoke. The truth of it all dawned brightly on the traveler. Jesus was the promised Messiah. His crucifixion did not diminish that fact. What the eunuch read in Isaiah only enhanced it.

The two passed a river. Some claim it is the Wadi el-Hesi northeast of Gaza. It is anybody's guess. When the Ethiopian saw the water, his enthusiasm bubbled over. "What prevents me from being baptized right now?" he asked. He believed and evidently told Philip how he felt.

In the New Testament, there is no argument for or

against water baptism. It is a foregone conclusion. Do you believe? Then demonstrate it by being baptized. This was the normal, accepted way of identifying with Jesus Christ and the new life.

Philip was just as enthused as the new believer. "Stop the chariot. Let's do it."

How can a Christian disciple receive a eunuch as a full brother in Christ? Philip merely continued this magnificent practice of acceptance. Men, women, Jews, Gentiles, foreigners can all come to Christ as they are. The eunuch has no restrictions. He doesn't carry a special stamp which makes him a second-class or conditional brother. Every door stands wide open.

It is an insult to the name of Christ wherever such an open door policy doesn't exist today. Some churches still reject people on the basis of race or background. It is a strange system which would have been foreign to Philip.

The evangelist left the eunuch immediately after the baptism. The Spirit took him away but we don't know how. Was he whisked through the air? Did he jump the next chariot heading north? Maybe he felt compelled to leave and merely walked away.

Either way, his job was finished. He had traveled a possible fifty miles simply to talk to one man. As he left, he must have been whistling a happy tune.

Philip was next found twenty miles north at Azotus, the old city of Ashdod. There he shared the gospel as he did at practically every city he visited. On this trip he preached all the way back to Caesarea.

The deacon may have settled down at Caesarea. Eventually he became a family man there. The last time we find him in the Scriptures, he is the proud father of four daughters. Each had become an evangelist. They are sharing the same gospel of Christ which their father spent his life spreading (Acts 21:8). Paul stopped off to see the veteran warrior when he visited the area.

Philip was the epitome of an excellent Christian spirit. Not out to gain fame for himself, he cut new ground in the name of a risen Saviour.

Something To Think About

1. Is money overemphasized in your Christian groups? Do you feel bombarded with appeals? Is money collecting being abused by some groups? Explain.
2. Why did you become a Christian? Was a miracle involved before your decision? What do you feel is the most effective way to share the gospel?
3. What do you personally think about miracles today?
4. Do you feel Simon was a Christian? Explain.
5. Do present-day Christians suffer persecution? Does persecution help or hurt the church?
6. Should the gospel be spread mostly in urban or rural areas? Does it make any difference?
7. Do we still discriminate against people of other races and backgrounds? How can we help the situation?

7
CORNELIUS

A Gentleman, He Paved The Way for You and Me

A man of cool confidence, Cornelius was a successful officer in the Roman army stationed at Caesarea. He had responsibility, recognition, and more money than the average person. It is correct to say he commanded respect. Considerable power was in his grasp if he decided to use it.

Cornelius was miles from home, but he was accustomed to being away. Because the Roman armies occupied several nations, the soldiers moved often. Some officers were cruel and uptight; others were kind and fair. Cornelius fit into the second category.

While he was generous to the people where he occupied, his philanthropy could not be confused with weakness. His love for his emperor and the empire was paramount. If he had to wield the sword, Cornelius wouldn't hesitate.

He appears to be well-rounded and secure. No thirst for petty vindictiveness. No need to exercise violence just to flex his muscles.

As a centurion, Cornelius had 100 men under his command, and commanded considerable weight over the foot soldier and local population. Six of these 100-man groups together were called a cohort. Cornelius' cohort bore the title of the Italian band. When ten of the cohorts were together they were called a legion, with a strength of 6,000.

Centurions are mentioned in the New Testament without a derogatory remark. The first centurion mentioned lived in Capernaum. He had a magnanimous spirit. A considerate man, he loved the nation of Israel and contributed heavily to build the local synagogue.

We don't dare lose the significance of this. Capernaum was in Galilee. In this region there were large numbers of rebels and zealots. They often attacked Roman soldiers and were continually fighting for their freedom. In this tense territory it would have been doubly hard to relax and be kind. Nevertheless, this professional soldier managed to earn respect. The Jews who knew him spoke highly of the centurion. They recommended him to Jesus strenuously.

Jesus responded to the plea by healing the centurion's servant who was nearly dead. This is the first Gentile to enter the ministry of Jesus Christ (Luke 7:1-10).

Later it was a centurion who stood by the cross and said, "Truly this was the Son of God" (Matthew 27:54b).

Cornelius fell into the same mix as the other noble centurions. He possessed a devotion to God and was open about it. Those who made up his household shared his enthusiasm for the spiritual and eternal.

Though he had a healthy portion of human

strength, Cornelius realized there is more to life than money, power, servants, and prestige. They were not the qualities which satisfied. Communication with the Heavenly Father was needed to make him complete.

Normally the centurion was under considerable strain. He was the muscle of the Roman army. If he didn't function correctly, the cohort and legion were useless. In most cases he rose through the ranks. A member of the ordinary class, the average centurion had distinguished himself and was noted for his ability. Courage was the most prominent quality. If they were attacked, the centurion was expected to hold his ground or die trying.

The centurion's specific duties covered three areas. He was responsible for the discipline of his troops. This is why the centurion had a vine staff as his emblem. When necessary, he used it on his men. Under some circumstances he not only beat his men but could execute them.

A second responsibility was to keep the troops in shape. They had to drill regularly. The centurion administered regular inspections and had final jurisdiction over supplies.

His most important function came due in battle itself. Once there, he was totally responsible for the performance of his men.

It was into the life of a friendly centurion that God decided to move mysteriously. God was bridging the chasm between the Jews and the Gentiles. He wanted to demonstrate His love to both equally.

Cornelius received an open vision during the early evening. An angel of God startled him—fearless soldier or not. The centurion stared at his visitor with his eyes riveted. He knew he wasn't dreaming. He was wide awake and healthy. Immediately Cornelius asked, "What is it, Lord?" (Acts 10:4b).

Two ingredients are obvious in the man: He is open, and he is willing. He is a creative adventurer. Most of us would probably still be taking aspirin and hoping the vision would go away. Cornelius, for all his surprise, *expects* God to do unusual things. From the beginning he accepts this as a message from God.

Certainly God is capable of giving visions today. Most of us will never see a vision, but the principle of communication has to remain vital. God can speak to us, both individually and collectively. He has done it regularly throughout history. Maybe it comes as a silent "leading"; to someone else it is a voice. At other times it is a circumstance. Certainly it comes through the Scriptures. If we believe God will not communicate, we probably have all our gates shut anyway. Christians who believe it could happen are more likely to feel a definite leading.

The angel announced God's intention to reward dedicated service. Because Cornelius' prayers and alms were given to the honor of God, they had been accepted. In response, God would bestow something special on his servant.

Almsgiving seems to ring a special bell with God. While many of us may have put it on a back burner, the Bible treats it with enormous warmth. The Old Testament spelled out definite guidelines for helping the poor. The compassion of the Israelites was well known and in sharp contrast to the nations surrounding them.

A needy person could enter any field and eat if he was destitute (Deuteronomy 23:24, 25). Farmers were forbidden to clean off their fields at harvest—the corners of the fields were left so the needy could stock up (Leviticus 23:22). An Israelite could not charge interest on money loaned to a poor person (Leviticus 25:35, 36).

When Jesus began His ministry, He carried over the same generous attitude. He told the Pharisees they should forget the sticky mechanics of the law. They would be far better off if they could keep the spirit of the law and give to the poor (Luke 11:41).

He had little patience with armchair theologians. What merit was there to keeping all the festivals if you really didn't care about people?

After the parable of the rich young fool Christ told His disciples to sell what they had and give alms (Luke 12:16 ff).

Cornelius saw giving as being at the heart of loving God. He proved he cared and God decided to put His seal of approval on it.

God wanted to explain the gospel of Jesus Christ to a Gentile soldier. Then, why didn't He? Why didn't the angel of the Lord merely tell Cornelius the good news? Instead he explained a series of steps he could take to discover the truth.

There seem to be two reasons why God didn't tell him directly. One is that He has chosen people to carry His Word. We are basically the hands, feet and voice of God in this world (Matthew 28:19). The second reason for going through these steps is to keep His followers in unity (John 17). He definitely did not want a Jewish church and a Gentile church. It was important that they become one from the beginning.

Cornelius' instructions were clear. He was to send men to Joppa (today it is annexed to Tel Aviv). There they were to find Simon Peter. Simon was staying by the seashore in the house of Simon the tanner. The directions seemed adequate, so the angel left.

The centurion was accustomed to taking orders and giving them. Without another word, he set the plan into action. Cornelius summoned two house servants and one soldier. The three would make the one-day journey south and find the sparkling apostle.

The soldier Cornelius selected for the trip is described as a devout or godly man. There is something contagious about this type of righteousness. It doesn't seem pretentious or bogged down with painful weights. The dedication of this threesome seemed sincere and proved even more so later.

So far this historic meeting was moving like a picnic in June. Everything was just right. Now God had to do His work on the Joppa side.

To understand what was about to take place, we have to appreciate Peter's background. He had always been taught that a person could come to God only by being a Jew. But Christ had now come, and Peter was having trouble sorting all of this out. Does a Gentile have to become a Jew before he can become a Christian? So far only Gentile Jews had come to be baptized. Cornelius' party was on its way to help clear Peter's mind.

For the moment at least, the matter seemed clear to Peter. Of course one must become a Jew before he can become a Christian. In God's effort to open Peter's mind, he used the same form of communication he used for Cornelius. While praying on a housetop, Peter went into a trance and saw a vision (Acts 10:10-15).

In the vision, a white sheet descended from

heaven. It was held up mysteriously at the four corners. Inside the sheet was a large assortment of four-footed beasts, birds and creeping things.

A voice said, "Peter, kill and eat." Peter objected because some of the animals were not clean. The voice then said, "What God hath cleansed, that call not thou common." The voice spoke a third time and the sheet pulled back up into heaven. How bewildering can a vision be? Peter stroked his beard and scratched his scalp. Fortunately, he wasn't left too long to ponder. While he struggled, three men from Caesarea arrived outside the tanner's gate. The Spirit of God spoke directly to Peter. He was to go with this visiting trio and ask no questions. Everything would work out fine.

The fiery apostle was molded from the same cast as Cornelius. He bounced right over to the gate and introduced himself. They were to spend the night with him. The next day they would all take off for wherever. God didn't have to tell Peter twice.

In the morning Peter collected some of his Christian friends and both parties left Joppa together. They spent one day on the road and arrived at Caesarea. What an adventure. God had mapped out a plan and they were eager to follow it.

Cornelius was waiting, high with excitement. He had gathered his relatives and close friends. It is safe to assume he had been sharing Christ regularly with practically everyone he knew. He may have had a churchless church meeting in his home.

It would have been fascinating to know what they were studying. Were they reading some form of the Old Testament? Did they pray in ignorance and ask God for guidance? Were they merely swapping opinions and wading aimlessly? Whatever the process, their sincerity was undebatable. God decided to honor their honest search for Him.

When Cornelius saw Peter coming, he ran to the apostle and fell at his feet. It is interesting to see how humble this officer was. He appeared to be a living definition of true meekness. Cornelius had the strength to demand and command. He also had the humility to take suggestions, serve and show respect for others. Courage and pliability were his golden combination.

Meekness has received a bad name, but actually it is a heroic quality. Jesus Christ told us the meek will inherit the world (Matthew 5:5). Frankly, this is an embarrassment to many of us. We picture ourselves as confident and decisive. Meek sounds retiring and cowardly.

Jesus Christ called Himself meek and lowly in heart (Matthew 11:29). There is no need to explain meekness away. It is a noble quality which allows us to serve other people and learn from them.

Sometimes Christians, in their eagerness to share their faith, lose their humility. We are so proud to be children of the king. If we are not careful, we come across as arrogant rather than helpful.

Cornelius had a good comprehension of the Word and its spirit. He didn't have to bow down or even cooperate—he could have demanded his own way but declined to do so. This is what made him workable in the hands of God.

Peter correctly resisted Cornelius' worship. No one knew better than the apostle that he was like everyone else. This didn't detract from the officer's attitude, however. He was grateful and not too proud to admit it.

This historic meeting needs a little explanation. Both men seemed a little ill at ease. Peter explained how he happened to come to a Gentile centurion—highly irregular to be sure. Jews and Gentiles didn't normally mix too well. Cornelius outlined his background and described the vision he had had three or four days before.

Peter had come to teach Cornelius, but he had a surprise in store. The Roman officer was about to take a giant step toward changing the apostle's life. Peter summed up the situation immediately: "Of a truth I perceive that God is no respecter of persons" (Acts 10:34b).

This may seem like an easy lesson to us, but it was actually quite a revelation. Later, Peter would defend God's impartiality to the council at Jerusalem (Acts 15), and still later he would again have second thoughts (Galatians 2:11).

Christ had developed a reputation for impartiality. He ministered to people from all walks and nationalities. This had become such a notable part of His lifestyle that His critics made fun of Him. When the chief priests and scribes wanted to trap Jesus, they sent spies with tricky questions. When they wanted to ensnare Him, they started with a backhand compliment: "Master, we know that thou sayest and teachest rightly, neither acceptest thou the person of any, but teachest the way of God truly" (Luke 20:21). They knew He didn't respect favored people. However, they clearly thought He should.

At least for the moment the light broke open brightly on Peter. He explained the complete gospel of Jesus Christ to a Gentile Roman commander.

Peter was carrying out a full service to God which he himself did not entirely understand.

While Peter was explaining the gospel, the Holy Spirit fell on Cornelius and his household—a clear indication that they eagerly believed what they had heard. The evidence of the Spirit was obvious as the Gentiles began to speak in tongues.

There is some justification for calling this the Gentile Pentecost. The events are similar to those from Acts 2. The reason seems well-planned. Gentiles had to enter the church on the same level as the Jews. If there was any hint that the Gentiles were second-rate Christians, the damage would be enormous. Equal footing was the only possible acceptable level. God was carefully carving out His church.

Peter immediately called for the baptism of the new believers. Exactly like Pentecost, there was no waiting period between acceptance and baptism. While many arguments are offered today for a trial period prior to baptism, they certainly were not prominent in Acts.

Cornelius and his friends leaned on Peter and his company to stay with him. For a few days they continued to swap experiences and Christian doctrine.

The news spread like warm butter. Soon ears were buzzing in Judea and not all of the comments were favorable. Some Christians were, frankly, shocked. How could Peter have met with Gentiles and then told them they were Christians? What kind of decay had invaded the church? It was transparent desecration. The Jews now had social contact and fellowship with pagans; they had cheapened the gospel by making it available to everyone. Some Christians would never get over it.

When Peter arrived at Jerusalem he carefully explained what had happened. He didn't want gossip to complicate the facts. Luke, the author of Acts, who has stated the problem and its progress, now drops the subject at this point (Acts 11:18). Later he again discusses it, depicting the deep troubles which resulted from the acceptance of Gentile Christians, but for the time being the problem is settled.

Fortunately for everyone, the first Gentile convert was a man of Cornelius' stature. It probably made no difference that he was a soldier or centurion; however, it was terribly important to find him a gentleman. An obnoxious personality like Simon the sorcerer (Acts 8:9 ff) or a deceptive couple like Ananias and Sapphira (Acts 5:1 ff) could have proven disastrous.

Despite what we sometimes hear, there are people who seek after God. Their motives and lives may not be pure, but their desire is real. In Cornelius we see this type of person. His was not merely an intellectual quest. The Roman centurion had a heart hungry for God.

Something To Think About

1. Were you searching for God when you became a Christian? Did God find you when you were disinterested?

2. Do we as Christians have an open attitude toward God's leading in our lives? Are we creative and adventurous as Cornelius was? Are we uptight and too careful?

3. Is almsgiving prominent among your group of Christian friends? Why are some distrustful of helping the poor?

What is the present trend among Christians?
4. Does God speak to people apart from other people? What about through nature?
5. Would we find it difficult to accept certain ethnic and economic backgrounds in our Christian groups? Explain.
6. Does your church group baptize immediately or have a waiting period? Why?

8
DORCAS

Cheerful and Generous, She Experienced A Miracle

The entire day has been a disaster. People have disappointed us. We have spun our wheels and gotten nowhere. The whole world seems like a bummer. Then someone drops by with a smile as clear as a clean window.

Our friend is always up. Show him a pile of garbage and he discusses the value of worms. On a rainy day he talks about the relief his garden will get. We have all met people like that.

In a nutshell, we have just described Dorcas. Herod is remembered for his cruelty. Judas is recalled for his betrayal. Dorcas survives in our memory because she was never afraid to be kind and giving.

Dorcas was like a dogwood tree in May. She was refreshing and carried a fragrance of hope. You just knew that if there were people like her around, there was a bright prospect for tomorrow.

Other than her devotion to God and mankind, we

know little about Dorcas. Eight verses cover her whole life in the Scriptures. Dorcas lived in Joppa (part of Tel Aviv). She was a Christian, but we don't know when she became one. Her Greek friends called her Dorcas, but her Hebrew friends used the name Tabitha. Both of them mean gazelle.

There is no reason to believe she ever read the book of James, but she could have written it. Her favorite verse could have been, "But wilt thou know, O vain man, that faith without works is dead?" (James 2:20).

Eventually Dorcas went the way of all flesh and died. We don't know the cause of her death; it was likely a natural event. But many people probably had a part of their heart chipped away when she died. The mourning was widespread and sincere.

Dorcas may have been a widow or single; still, she didn't lack for anyone to care for her body. In all probability her friends responded to the task. They prepared her body for the funeral.

Most Jewish families tried to adhere to certain guidelines concerning funerals. Embalming was almost unheard of except with Jacob and Joseph. Cremation was practiced in some nations, but rejected by the Jews. Usually the body was thoroughly washed, then wrapped in linen and perfumes.

The body was usually buried the day the death occurred (Deuteronomy 21:23). Some groups still keep this rule today. Often the body was placed in a cave or tomb and allowed to decompose. After a period of time the bones were placed into an ossuary box. This container could be kept in a tomb or other suitable place.

These were probably the plans for Dorcas' body. After she was cleansed and wrapped, she was placed in an upper chamber. This chamber was usually either a second story room or a room on the upstairs porch. Friends would come to mourn and pay their final respects. In some cases, professional mourners would be hired.

When the Christian community at Joppa heard that Peter was in nearby Lydda, they decided to send quickly for his help. They loved Dorcas greatly and wanted to try and assist her if at all possible. Lydda was only nine miles from Joppa, so the trip could be made in about half a day.

When did they send for Peter? In all probability, her friends started the trip while she was sick and fading. They loved her and believed in miracles. They also believed in special apostolic authority. Peter could do something to restore her health. He had performed other miracles.

Dorcas had taught her friends a valuable lesson. When you love someone, you do something to demonstrate it. Words are nice and are essential to good communication, but action is love with arms.

It is interesting to see how Jesus handled the need for love in His own life. On several occasions He asked His friends if they loved Him. Why did He really care? He was the Son of God. Jesus had intimate fellowship with the God of the universe. What did it really matter if a handful of fishermen loved Him?

Christ understood the need for love because He was a full personality. Since He was capable of giving love He could also receive it.

It is also good to see His definition of love. If His friends loved Him, they would do what pleased Him. If they didn't love Christ, they would ignore Him.

Love has arms.

This is why the King James translation rendered the word love as charity in I Corinthians 13. Charity meant to do something. Love which is sterile is incomplete. Love which is mature does something for the person it loves. Christ understood this. Dorcas understood. Dorcas' friends were grasping the same reality.

Sometime after the party left to find Peter, Dorcas died. Those who had ministered to her were crushed. Their close and generous friend was gone. The weeping and preparing began.

When the traveling group arrived at Lydda they quickly found Peter and pressed on him. He had to come; they were pleading the case of a close friend. Surely God did not want her to die. Dorcas did too much good; she spread too much happiness and hope.

Peter was impressed with the emergency of the situation and left immediately. There was no time for explanation. Time was extremely important. When he arrived at Joppa, Peter was taken directly to the upper chamber. The trophies to Dorcas' goodness dotted the room. Widows stood with coats and garments draped over their arms. These were the articles of clothing she had made for the people she loved.

It was particularly appropriate to see widows in the room. Throughout Christ's ministry and the early church, widows held a special place in the hearts of Christians.

Christ came to their defense early when He condemned the Pharisees for taking advantage of them. Widows were often vulnerable. The men were better trained in trade and commerce. If a widow had no close relatives to help protect her, she could easily be cheated. Evidently they were swindling widows out of their money in the name of God and charity (Mark 12:40).

The Hebrews always had a special protection for their widows. They considered God their particular guardian. When they asked, "How do you tell a righteous man?" the answer was easy. A righteous person cares for the widows (Psalm 146:9).

When James asked for the definition of true religion the answer was easy to a real Jew. True religion was to visit the fatherless and the widows (James 1:27). This is why Paul gives such careful instructions on ministering to widows. It had to be done correctly and fairly across the board, but by all means it had to be done (I Timothy 5:3 ff).

The widows who circled the upper room were living testimonials to Dorcas' interpretation of God's guidance. The unpretentious seamstress from Joppa had carried it out to perfection.

Dorcas had personally made the coats and garments which draped those in the room. Through most of history it has been painstaking to make clothing. We don't know exactly how Dorcas did it, but we are certain it involved a great deal of work. Cloth was often made of flax and cotton. After spinning, these were woven into pieces of cloth of all sizes. Other materials were made from woven wool gathered from sheep. A few had leather clothing.

Often the materials were dyed from berries and other color sources. These homemakers were not as bland as some might think. They often made clothing with multiple and bright colors.

These woven materials were then sewn by hand.

The seamstress could work rapidly with a needle and an awl. Many of the ladies were adroit at using these tools. Even women of rank usually joined in the process of making clothes.

Dorcas made things to give away. Some people are still excellent at this avenue of kindness. They are continuously sewing clothes, dolls and quilts to give away. This lady did it with a passion and determination. The widows brought these gifts with them now as a final tribute to Dorcas.

When Peter assessed the situation he lost no time in going to work. The first step was to clear the room. Everyone, widows and mourners, would have to leave. This was the same thing Jesus did when He raised Jairus' daughter. Peter couldn't be expected to be an expert in resurrection, so he had to depend on what he had seen.

As usual, Peter must be credited with courage and a rare quality called audacity. What experience did the apostle have in the fine art of resurrection? But he did have a healthy mixture of faith and daring. While others would still be thinking it over and chewing their fingernails, Peter jumped in.

With great simplicity and direction he said, "Tabitha, arise." No tricks or gimmicks. He didn't even use a medium like dirt or a handkerchief. Just, "Dorcas, it's time to get up."

Her eyes moved like a venetian blind. A miracle had occurred: Dorcas was alive.

There may be no definite guidelines for miracles, but that doesn't diminish their reality. Some people in the Bible were healed because they had enormous faith. Others were healed because the administrator had great faith. Still others seemed to experience miracles only because God had faith.

It would be tidy to set out immovable laws which govern miracles. But nothing that neat really exists. The only dependable rule is that God is the great administrator. We are invited to ask. He holds the prerogative to act or withhold.

The story of Dorcas is a high tribute not only to her but to women in general. There are several places where these accolades show up in the Bible. One of the most significant chapters is Romans 16, where Paul closes his epistle by commending a number of helpful women. Some had been like quiet cargo ships in the night. Some had been bold and exercised leadership, but all had given excellent support.

The apostle makes special note of Phebe, a Christian who lived in Cenchrea. This was an important port seven miles east of Corinth. Phebe had those two superior qualities for which Dorcas was praised: First, she was a believer who had cast her lot with Jesus Christ; and second, she had amazing generosity. Paul succinctly says Phebe was a helper of many, including the apostle.

This is the first mention of a woman deacon in the church. Phebe was servant (Romans 16:1), which can be translated deacon, or deaconess. It described both a service and an office.

Doubtless, they continued the noble Christian tradition of helping widows. Often they were widows themselves. But their ministry stretched much beyond widows. Paul also fell within the pale of their kindness and generosity.

In Romans 16, we are also reintroduced to an active woman, Priscilla, and her husband, Aquila. Their involvement in the gospel work had been so extensive that they risked their lives for the apostle. They now have a church which meets regularly in their home.

Mary receives a short but sincere notice. She, too, had worked hard for the cause of Christ (verse 6).

Paul can't forget to mention the mother of Rufus. She had been such a fine lady, almost like Paul's own mother (verse 13).

There may be other women listed in this group. Some of their names are difficult to ferret out. But just this sampling gives us a good idea of the high opinion and appreciation Paul held for women. The modern debate over whether Paul hated women should be silenced here.

Christ set a fantastic example for the elevation of women. He included women among His personal friends.

Mary Magdalene was a woman who had been possessed by seven demons. They had vacated and now she was a committed supporter of Christ. Mary contributed financially to Jesus' ministry in Galilee. She traveled with the troop of disciples as did Joanna and Susanna (Luke 8:1-3). Her status as a woman did not deter Christ from befriending and incorporating her into His work.

A certain class of people were insulted by Jesus' companionship with women. Some held to extremely rigid rules concerning women. But not everyone. In some Jewish circles women were given tremendous latitude (Proverbs 31).

Mary of Bethany and her sister Martha also played a considerable part in Christ's life. Their personalities were different. Mary appears to be a serious thinker who often took time out to contemplate. Martha was strictly busy hands. Jesus visited in their home and didn't allow Himself to become upset when His critics couldn't understand why He would allow a woman to anoint Him.

These were the more obvious women who ministered in Christ's life. Several others pop up in the Scriptures now and then.

Women have always taken a major responsibility in the presentation of the gospel. Dorcas was but one example of their excellence. Today many continue to live the full extent of genuine service to Christ.

Something To Think About

1. What are "good works" to you? Are they on the increase or decrease in your Christian circles?
2. What part do "good works" play in the Christian life? Are they overemphasized?
3. What is your definition of love? Can you love a person and not show it? Explain.
4. What are the biggest needs of widows in your community? How can your church or group be of the best help to them?
5. How do you picture the role of women in the early church? How does it compare with their present role?
6. Compare Christ's attitude toward women with ours. Was He more open than we are? Was He less?

9
JAMES

At First Skeptical, He Became a Stalwart Leader

What would it have been like to grow up with Jesus Christ? He had brothers and sisters living under the same roof, and sometimes it must have been hard. If we think it was difficult growing up with our siblings, imagine if one of them had been perfect. Every time we got into trouble we would become all the angrier at the one who didn't.

There is a great deal we don't know about this carpenter's home at Nazareth. However, there are a few pieces we can put together. We do know it was a laboring class home. They may not have lived in desperate poverty, but neither were they well off.

Jesus had four younger half-brothers: James, Joseph, Judas and Simon. He also had an unknown number of half-sisters (Matthew 13:54-56). There is some possibility they are the older children of Joseph. It is more likely they are the younger children of Mary. This adds a little color to our picture. Jesus was brought up in a home with six to eight half-brothers and sisters. Money may have been sufficient, but it could not have been plentiful.

There is no reason to believe they didn't get along as children. They may have been the happiest family north of Jerusalem. There are only two quiet strains which may indicate stress. The first was a sinless sibling. Some days that may not have gone down well. The second indication is the reluctance of the brothers and sisters to believe. They frankly didn't think He was who He claimed to be.

The James we find in Acts 15 is one of these brothers. Another James, who was a disciple, was executed by order of Herod (Acts 12:2). The brother James went through some agonizing moments before he could accept Jesus as the Messiah.

The negative feelings of His brothers came out during Christ's ministry at the time of the feast of the tabernacles. Jesus had stayed clear of Judea because the opposition had become so heated, but a trip to Jerusalem seemed in order for the feast. Jesus, however, decided to skip this observance and stay in Galilee.

At this point His brothers began taunting Him. They thought He should go south and show Himself. In essence, they were telling Him to take His magic act to Judea.

His family may have been embarrassed by the commotion Jesus was causing. The miracles, crowds, and all the strange sayings were not the attention they wanted. The best thing might be for Him to spend more time in Judea. At this point His brothers weren't about to believe in Him (John 7:5).

These few short glimpses are all we see of the family. From them we gather a loose skeleton and collect a few feelings. How deeply these emotions run is hard to say.

They should be an encouragement to everyone who feels a strain in family relationships. These feelings are regrettable, but not uncommon. Wherever there are the dynamics of human beings, there is the potential for friction. Some of it existed in the family of Jesus Christ. He knows exactly how you feel.

Something happened to the family of Christ between this Judean debate and His resurrection. None of the Gospel writers has supplied us the details. Maybe the brothers started listening more carefully. Possibly His arrest and crucifixion had a telling effect on their lives.

Whatever the cause, the outcome is obvious. After the resurrection of Christ we find a group of believers waiting in an upper room in Jerusalem. Among the believers are Mary, Jesus' mother, and His brethren (Acts 1:14). Something dramatic and life-changing has happened. Probably the best clue is passed on to us by Paul. The apostle tells us James saw the resurrected Christ (I Corinthians 15:7). If His brother had not yet believed, this historical event must have sealed the evidence. From this point, James was willing to give his life for the brother he never before quite understood.

Immediately James was accepted by his fellow Christians as a capable leader. His personal sighting of the risen Saviour gave him special standing with the group. Paul referred to him as an apostle in the same sense as the others in that marked circle.

Why did James rise so quickly as a prominent leader in the early church? Was it because of his sincere dedication and service? There is no doubt these qualities were evident in his life. However, there also may have been an added respect because he was the brother of Jesus Christ. It certainly had to catch everyone's attention. Paul clearly noted this distinction in Galatians 1:19, "But other of the apostles saw I none, save James the Lord's brother."

If we were in the same room with the brother of the President, all of us would soon be aware of it. In all likelihood the relationship widened James' ministry.

There is some possibility that James tried to downplay the family ties. When he wrote his excellent epistle he described himself in the simplest of terms. He referred to himself as a threefold servant of God, Jesus Christ and the scattered tribes of Israel (James 1:1). James doesn't choose to exploit being a brother of Christ.

James maintained a ministry among the Jews. As the ministry of the disciples widened, many took the gospel to Gentile nations. For whatever reason, James saw his special talents as more suitable among his own people.

The next time we find James, he holds a significant role in the church at Jerusalem (Acts 15). An enormously important council was held in that city around A.D. 45. The most famous figures in the early church gathered to settle a murderous problem. Peter, Paul, John, Barnabas and James were among the renowned characters who had assembled. At this time Jerusalem was still considered the mother church and hub of the wheel.

No council in history has been more important than this one. The question of Gentile acceptance was a dramatic scene which tried the church in its infancy. If they failed this test, its ministry would be drastically changed and limited. Each of us can praise God that the debate ended as well as it did. Otherwise we would all be carrying heavy burdens, still trying to please God.

James played a leading role in steering the church correctly. If he had backed off here, the gospel would have been weakened considerably. The whole discussion began because Paul and Barnabas were highly successful in their ministry to the Gentiles. Churches were being established and non-Jews were packing in.

Inevitably the paramount question arose: Don't these Gentiles have to become Jews before they can become Christians? At the heart of this debate was circumcision. Some believers said an uncircumcised person was unsaved whether Christ died for his sins or not (Acts 15:1).

Paul and Barnabas were beside themselves. They weren't going to allow these shackles to be placed on the new converts. When they arrived at Jerusalem they shared their good report with the apostles and elders. God was clearly performing a remarkable miracle.

But some Christians couldn't share in their enthusiasm. They were believers who had come from the Pharisaic branch of Judaism. Their conversions had been genuine, but many had brought their legalistic mentality with them. They still saw God as a picky perpetrator of petty laws.

Since their conversion, they had loosened up considerably. Their old friends wouldn't have recognized them. They were so much more open-minded. The grace of God had left its mark on their lives, but still, they could only go so far. Surely God had not dismissed the entire Old Testament law.

Throwing out circumcision was like nullifying the Ten Commandments. Now, in the viewpoint of some, Christians were turning their liberty into lunacy.

Legalism has always been a sore spot in the Christian community. What makes it doubly dangerous is that no one admits to being guilty. Ask anyone if he is a legalist and he will tell you no. It's too horrid for any sane person to admit to. No church will name itself the North Bank Legalistic Church. These are creatures which have become extinct, yet we are surrounded by them.

The early Christians needed to thrash this problem out. Ever since then we too have had to struggle with the same concept. Legalism is to believe that God will show favor on us if we keep certain rules. These rules are usually arbitrary and selected by the legalist, but he refuses to admit this. As far as he is concerned each law came directly from the Scriptures—more or less.

We still try to infringe on people's lives in the name of righteousness. We feel strongly about something and we are going to get our two cents in. Legalism is telling people what they can wear or how many services they must attend. At other times it's telling a person how much he has to give. It may be trying to control a divorced woman's life.

The process is void of grace. It usually is sick from a lack of love. Attitudes and understanding are at a minimum. Judgment and condemnation are riding high.

The Christian Pharisees probably wanted to break out of this pattern. Certainly they had come a long way, but some concepts of freedom were merely beyond them. Paul was an exception. The apostle was proud to be a Pharisee, as was his father (Acts 26:5; 23:6). But his mind had made a drastic flip. He now saw legalism as an enemy of the cross of Christ (Galatians 2:19). Some think Paul wrote Galatians prior to this council and that it added considerable fuel to the fire.

Peter is a perfect example of the agonizing man in the middle. When he met with the council at Jerusalem, the fisherman was sold on liberty. Later on, Peter vacillated again.

Doubtless there were several impassioned speeches on both sides of the aisle. Luke doesn't record all of them but Peter's plea was so impressive it couldn't be overlooked. Peter had come a long way and presently was in favor of taking Gentiles into the church immediately.

He testified how he personally had preached to non-Jews and was convinced God was working among them (Acts 15:7-11). Paul and Barnabas then took the floor and added measurably to the theme. The audience sat silently, some of them hearing evidence they had never before considered.

Then James moved forcefully to the lead. He completely agreed with his fellow apostles. The Pharisaic issue could not prevail. James' exact position with the group is unclear. Some believe he was president of the council. Certainly he received tremendous respect.

All of these men, and James in particular, deserve a great deal of credit for taking a stand. Their personal feelings and reputations had to be expendable. If they failed, Christianity was destined to be a Jewish sect. This was the way the pagan world now looked at them. If they failed this test, they would never be able to shake off this shadow.

Two points were paramount in the discussion: Was the church of Jesus Christ to be a universal ministry, or only directed to a limited segment? The second question was personal acceptance: Were Jewish Christians going to allow Gentiles into the church without Jewish restrictions?

James and his friend established an outstanding precedent. It was in the excellent tradition of Christ Himself. They decided to stick their necks out for the oppressed. Without regard for their personal popularity they expressed their feelings.

If you have ever been in the heat of a battle you can definitely appreciate what was happening. Those who sit on the fence while vital issues are being resolved make the matter painful. They share your feelings. They see clearly the import of the question. Yet, to protect their personal comfort and prestige, they prefer to say nothing. Thank God for those who know when to stand up and let their feelings out.

Christ's brother was not a crude head knocker. He made a proposal which would alleviate the situation and at the same time soothe Jewish consciences. But certain aspects could not be compromised. Circumcision could not be a prerequisite to salvation—Jesus Christ did not set this or any other stipulation. The apostles would be abusive if they tried to tie any clauses to the contract. There would be no initiation rites to becoming a Christian. Thanks, James, for keeping the important issues clear.

However, liberty could not be allowed to degenerate into stupidity. There were some practices Gentiles should avoid to be kind to Jewish believers.

To begin with, they should avoid meat which had been offered to idols if a Jewish Christian was near. There was nothing wrong with the food. The meat usually was sold or otherwise shared. For Gentile Christians it was a simple matter. The idols couldn't eat it and since they were dead stones, they couldn't even contaminate it. After it had been placed in front of lifeless statues, there was no sense in throwing good meat away—they might as well eat it. But the Jewish Christians couldn't see it quite as innocently. To them it had been offered to a pagan deity. Whether the deity was real or phony was not the point.

James agreed with the Gentiles. The meat didn't mean anything. But they needed to learn another important lesson: Avoid hurting fellow Christians. Gentiles, when your Jewish friends come over for supper, don't serve the temple meat. Save it for picnics with your relatives.

The second plank in James' advice was a hot coal. Most people who pick it up don't handle it for long. The Gentile Christians were encouraged to avoid fornication. But aren't all Christians naturally asked to do this? Why did James add it?

In the Gentile world the marriage relation was often in a shambles. Many looked at sexual exercises with the same lightness as we might consider tennis. They were less convinced of an abiding love between a man and a woman. Sexual exploits seemed to have little to do with pure or godly living.

If this was the reason (and it is a big if) we can understand what James was saying. Their lives were mixed up. They had intermarried and divorced and run around. But their lives were now changing in

Jesus Christ. They were not complete and there were entanglements which had to be resolved. During this period of realignment, they were to keep a low profile.

The Jews couldn't understand the changes the Gentiles were going through. Infidelity was foreign to most of them. The Gentile Christians knew what changes they had to make in most areas, though in some areas it was unclear. Play it cool until things are unscrambled, James was saying. This way the Jews will stay pacified and the new church can stay at relative peace.

The third concern was eating meat which did not have the blood properly drained. The Jews would not eat it unless it was. Gentiles saw no big deal. James said, Go ahead and eat it but don't flout it. Someday the Jewish Christians will be able to adapt.

First of all, remember the essential facts: You are free. Gentiles do not have to become Jewish or follow Jewish customs before they can become Christians. There will be no flinching or compromise.

The council in effect applauded James: We think you, James, have used excelling wisdom. Let's write it up and send the message to the local churches.

There is no record of opposition to the proposal, though we are safe in assuming there was some. Pharisaic mentalities did not normally surrender that easily. But if they objected further, they were swallowed up by Christian solidarity.

These men were taking a risk. But there is an inherent risk in the Christian life. They might be misunderstood. The Christian church might split immediately into Jewish and Gentile factions. James and his friends decided to take that chance. Unless the church stood up for truth, it wouldn't be worth preserving anyway.

The council selected two Jews and two Gentiles to deliver the message. They were to head directly for Antioch where it would be warmly appreciated.

James had come a long way. One day he was taunting his brother Jesus into going into dangerous Judea; now he was a great defender of the pure gospel by faith. His contribution to the church and its believers would be enormous both during his life and today.

Something To Think About

1. Is it more difficult to live a Christian life in our own home? Why do some adults find it hard to live out life in front of sisters and brothers?
2. What is your definition of legalism? Are there some ways in which we are Pharisees?
3. Do our churches or other groups place burdens on Christians which are not part of the gospel? Explain.
4. Do our churches need more rules or less? Give some examples.
5. How do you understand James' advice concerning adultery? Do we expect too much from new Christians?
6. Do you know Christians who are easily offended or touchy? How do they react to others?
7. Name some Christians you appreciate because of their courageous stand on issues. Do we suffer from too many believers merely going along? Explain.

10
SILAS

Quiet But Courageous, He Could Be Counted On

One man was on the scene when three different presidents were assassinated. Robert Todd Lincoln was close to his father, to Garfield, and to McKinley when each was felled. Like a silent ship cutting through the night, he called little attention to himself.

Silas reminds us of the same role. He will never play a big part in Biblical history, but he was there. More than an idle spectator, this gifted disciple was in the middle, working hard. Silas could remember wide-eyed audiences as they welcomed the gospel. He could also recall the cutting pain of a jailor's rod and the dank smell of a Roman prison.

We don't know where Silas came from. The first time we meet him is at the church in Jerusalem. He was well known and accepted by those who were meeting in special council. When this historic conference reached its conclusion (Acts 15:20, 21), they needed qualified men to distribute the news. Along with Paul and Barnabas, two local men, Silas and Judas Barsabas, were chosen to complete the assignment.

The party of four traveled immediately to Antioch where the debate over whether a Greek had to become a Jew to become a Christian had been especially hot. The newly-appointed quartet could hardly wait to get the word out.

Silas and Barnabas were particularly important to this trip. Since they had Greek blood and were respected by both sides, their presence would be reassuring to everyone. The response at Antioch was so appreciative it caught Silas immediately. He decided to settle down, at least for awhile, in Antioch.

Churches seem to have their own personalities. Some are rigid and demanding. Others are warm, welcoming and open-minded. One church is intent on preserving the old. The next is progressive and looking for new opportunities.

The church at Antioch possessed an embracing charm. Those who visited hated to leave. Barnabas and Paul had made a trip there to check it out and decided to stay awhile. Now Silas had smelled its fragrance and was mesmerized. The church worked like a magnet. If you got close to Antioch it pulled you in and you hated to leave.

Antioch was a new experiment which was working out wonderfully. Here pure Gentiles were believing in Jesus Christ as the Messiah and Saviour. Their background was not Jewish and yet they still accepted Christ. They were like clean slates waiting to be written on. There were no traditions to carry over. No one to stand up in a meeting, red-faced and steaming, to announce: "But we have always done it this way."

After Silas settled in Antioch, the missionaries began quarreling among themselves. Paul, Mark and Barnabas were having serious differences. We aren't exactly sure what placed them at odds, but we do know Paul was ready to go on a missionary journey and refused to take Mark (see chapters on Mark and Barnabas). Barnabas sided with Mark and the two went their way. Paul then selected Silas to join him.

Silas had to leave his Syrian oasis, but he didn't appear to resist. If he was needed, his spirit was eager. The duet took the northern tour through Asia Minor. They visited churches, taught, preached and tried to help wherever they could. Along the way they met an amazing young Christian named Timothy.

As Paul and Silas pushed northwest, a strange experience came over them. The Holy Spirit refused to let them preach as they traveled from region to region. We don't know how the Spirit communicated this, but it was obvious to them. Was it a feeling, an audible sound, a vision? We don't know, but the message was real. They moved out of Asia Minor without preaching another sermon.

The two showed a mature sensitivity. A special key to speaking is knowing when to be silent. Many of us would have been zealous beyond our intelligence. Those who are eager to speak will accept anything which comes their way. We act as if there is a peculiar righteousness to activity. We jump at any excuse to deliver three points and a poem. After all, it is flattering to be asked. It is ego building to weave a message in front of a collected audience. Sometimes the cash doesn't hurt either.

Point of fact: We don't fit into every situation.

Sometimes Christians are an embarrassment to everyone merely because they can't say no. Not every invitation is the voice of God. Sometimes it's the plea of a frustrated program chairman. Paul and Silas weren't hypnotized by the sound of their own voices.

The Spirit's command to start preaching again was as definite as the one to stop had been. While at Troas, Paul had a vision. In it a man from Macedonia stood praying. His prayer said, "Come over into Macedonia and help us" (Acts 16:9b).

Macedonia was a country north of Greece. Its most famous mountain was Olympus. Its chief cities were Philippi, Neapolis and Thessalonica. Paul could explain the vision in no other way than as a direct summons by God. The famous missionary hooked his arm around Silas and they were on their way. The ban had been lifted and they were like canaries getting over laryngitis.

It is hard to guess what they would have done if they had known what was waiting for them. Silas may have asked if he could return to beautiful Antioch. On the other hand, they might have doubled their pace.

Their first major destination, the impressive city of Philippi, was located on rich agricultural land and had become famous for its gold mines. Among its sites is the location of a famous battle. It was here that Antony and Octavian fought Brutus and Cassius, the assassins of Julius Caesar (42 B.C.).

Silas had to be impressed with this sophisticated city. It was an official Roman colony (Acts 16:12), therefore Philippi was governed by Roman law and its constitution was fashioned after the one in Rome.

Philippi was basically Roman in its thinking, although it also had a number of Jews. Naturally the apostles aimed directly for this group. There is no evidence of a synagogue, so the total number of Jews must have been small. They met each sabbath for prayer outside the city by the river. The group evidently consisted mostly of women who may have been married to Gentiles. Ten men were necessary to establish a synagogue and they were lacking some.

Silas and Paul met a fascinating character here named Lydia. She sold purple from Thyatira, an area famous for this material, and heard of the group which met by the river when she came to Philippi to sell the purple cloth she dyed.

Lydia listened to the message and chose to believe in Jesus Christ. She and her family agreed to be baptized and her conversion was immediately apparent. She was so happy with her new life she "pressed" on Paul and Silas to stay with her. The first convert in Europe learned Christian hospitality quickly.

We don't know how large a home Lydia owned or its exact location. It is possible she had servants and a sizeable estate. Whatever she possessed, it was open to the two disciples and they were greatly helped. It meant they wouldn't have to make tents for a living. They would have open time to spread the gospel. This was only the beginning of a strong relationship between the people of Philippi and the apostles. They would continue with financial support for years (Philippians 4:15, 16).

Was there any possible scandal in a woman befriending a number of male missionaries? Luke was also part of the group and we can only guess how many more. Of course they ran the risk of gossip.

Jesus Christ had been pelted with similar accusations. But three healthy cheers for Lydia and the missionaries—hospitality was daringly extended and daringly accepted. They could not suspend the guidelines of Christian living merely because some would not understand.

The impact of Christianity on Philippi had barely begun. Silas had bought a ticket to ride with Paul and they were just getting up speed. Hostility, miracles, pain, threats of death and amazing conversions were hiding around every corner. Silas was just beginning to enjoy the ride.

One day on the way to the river to pray, a young lady met them (Acts 16:16 ff). This woman was possessed by some unusual power. She had the spirit of Python or, literally, of Apollyon, which is the angel of the bottomless pit (Revelation 9:11). Voices would come from her over which she had apparently little control. She may have done several things, but one was to predict the future. The men who had charge of her made money by collecting for her services. They evidently made enough to consider her a valuable commodity.

The lady with the strange gifts started following Paul and Silas around. The voice inside her began crying out the truth, "These men serve the Most High God and proclaim to you the way of salvation" (see Acts 16:17).

Truer words were never spoken, but the source started to bother Paul. He must have felt this type of advertising was more harmful than helpful. Finally Paul became fed up with the ugly scene, pivoted and faced the woman. In the name of Jesus Christ he commanded the evil spirit to leave her. Almost without a whimper the spirit sheepishly evacuated. This again verifies the fact that, whatever we think of spirits taking over bodies, there is no question what Paul and Silas thought. They were convinced it was possible.

At this point we leave the scenic mountaintops and plummet toward the valley floor. If things have been pleasant and adventuresome, they are about to become frightening.

When the girl's masters heard of the spirit's sprint for freedom, they dropped their money bags. They had lost a franchise in the fortune-telling business. They pounced on Paul and Silas like linebackers after a fumble.

This was probably Silas' first experience at being dragged by the feet, but it wasn't even a novelty for Paul. He had been stoned and dragged out of Lystra some time earlier (Acts 14:19). Unfortunately, he would get the same mode of transportation later at Jerusalem (Acts 21:30). If it hadn't been for the tearing of skin and beating of his head, Silas could have looked at it as an educational experience.

Paul and Silas soon found themselves in front of the local magistrates. Under the Roman colony system, these were called praetors and resided in pairs. When the crowd made its accusations against the two, they may have thrown in a vicious twist. Their accusers called them Jews. Sometimes it was a title of respect. Probably in this case it was a demeaning smear. Jews have often been different. Among many people, to be different is a crime.

This is the reason so many Christians suffered in the early years. Rumors arose accusing them of all sorts of atrocious behavior because of their refusal to conform. Most of us have difficulty tolerating people who do not walk with our peculiar gait.

To guarantee religious conformity, the Romans passed laws forbidding certain propaganda. Only accepted forms of religion could be tolerated in their provinces. Paul and Silas were facing serious charges and they had little to recommend them. The magistrates tore the defendants' clothing and ordered the pair beaten.

It would be a mistake for us to consider this beating too lightly. The lictors who assisted the magistrates were highly professional. They carried both rods and an axe. Each was prepared to deal out corporal or capital punishment when called on.

We don't know how often they were hit with the rods. Under Jewish law it would have been 39 stripes; under the Roman system it is hard to know. The prosecution had an especially harsh hatred for the two. Sheer prejudice was evident in their choice of words. We can only imagine they were beaten with little regard for their lives.

Chalk up a new experience for Silas. Paul was destined to be beaten on two more occasions, but for Silas it was a new venture. There is no record he ever recommended it to others.

The two apostles were then thrown in jail. Not merely common prisoners, they were tossed into the inner prison—and the term "inner prison" is not used lightly here. Roman prisons had three main sections: the vestibule, the outer prison and the inner section.

"Inner prison" was a term calculated to send shivers up anyone's back. This section was literally a dungeon. The only light or air available had to rush in whenever the door opened. It was easily the worst treatment which could be given to a prisoner.

The jailer knew his job and went about it methodically. Creature comforts were not high on his list. His job description could be condensed to a short line: "Make sure they don't escape." With that theme overriding everything, he led each prisoner to the stocks.

Again, this is easy to dismiss lightly in a snug living room, but the stocks were miserable places designed to create the most agonizing pain. They were similar to the ones used in colonial America. There were several holes to hold the prisoners' legs. They could be spread far enough apart to guarantee continuous pain.

While sitting in this contorted position Silas had ample time to think the situation over. Why in the world was he sitting in a hopeless dungeon with his legs spread until his entire back ached? Because he had told a handful of women Jesus Christ died for them? Because a woman and her household had been baptized? Because a fortune-teller had a demon whisked out of her?

They sounded like slim reasons to incarcerate two grown men. But the gospel was important. If it could free some people, it was a threat to others. Silas was learning that lesson as he tried to rub circulation back into his limbs.

Prisons can sometimes make excellent laboratories—good places to test our theories and expand our minds. Paul and Silas decided they would never get a better chance to try healthy positive thinking than now. So around midnight they decided this was a good place to try their musical talents. After all, their audience, the other prisoners, had no choice but to listen. Besides, sucking their thumbs and feeling sorry for themselves wasn't the least bit productive. Singing sounded like a mind and soul saver.

With little timidity they opened their mouths and flexed their lungs. They were praying—not in a quiet corner as most of us do. Talking out loud to God seemed like a perfectly sane thing to do. If they added a few bars of music, it was all the better. Like lunatics who had snapped, they sat there as if they were leading a homecoming celebration.

We don't know how far away the other prisoners were, but they evidently could hear clearly. The word for listening indicates *pleasure*. Psalms were dancing off the dungeon walls where previously only curses and cries of pain had echoed.

Silas was now a member of a midnight duet. Being a missionary was too fast-moving to be dull.

In the middle of this musical interlude a terrific earthquake shook the prison. The picture is easy to see: When the walls were rocked apart, the bars separated. The chains ripped out of the walls. When the jailer recovered from the quake, he rushed quickly to the doors and found them wide open. He assumed the prisoners were gone.

The horrified soldier drew his sword and turned it to plunge the blade into his body. He couldn't live with defeat and saw suicide his only reasonable choice.

Paul, standing in the dark, shouted, "Don't hurt yourself, we are all here." Not one prisoner had escaped. Maybe they didn't have time; possibly they were still trying to climb out of the debris. At any rate, they were all there.

The jailer couldn't believe they were still in the

prison. Relieved, he ran to Paul and Silas, fell on his knees, and asked what he had to do to be saved. We don't really understand his question. Was he looking for physical salvation? Did he need protection from his superiors? Or did he recognize the spiritual qualities of the missionaries?

While we don't know the meaning of the question, we can be sure of the answer he was given. Paul and Silas told him to believe in Jesus Christ.

The jailer probably lived in the prison compound. He took the missionaries to meet his family. They also believed in Jesus Christ and were baptized that night.

This may not be the type of missionary work Silas had in mind, but strange things were happening. Not only was his life different in Christ, but even his instincts seemed to change. Most of us would have taken the first exit out of that prison. We could think about it later, but the thing to do was get moving. Silas, however, was becoming a new person. Life seemed to take on a fresh set of values. He decided to stay with Paul in that miserable prison.

The next day the magistrates had a change of heart. They didn't know if these Christians had anything to do with the earthquake, but they weren't taking any chances. Let them go. Get them out of the prison and town immediately.

We don't know how Silas felt about this sudden freedom, but Paul rejected it in a second. They had been arrested, tried and beaten publicly. They had no intention of now wiggling out of town quietly. The magistrates would have to come to the prison and personally escort them from the jail.

The officials were in no mood to argue. To make

matters worse, they discovered the prisoners were Roman citizens. They jogged directly to the jail and politely asked them to slide out of town. But Paul and Silas took their merry time. They visited the house of Lydia and renewed fellowship with the local believers. Then, at their own pace, they left Philippi.

Everyone was impressed—the non-believers, the new converts, and even Paul and Silas themselves. God had accomplished some remarkable things and had started a warm, lasting church in Philippi.

The roller coaster ride was far from over for Silas. At Thessalonica, crowds struck out against them and harassed those who were converted. Paul and Silas were forced to sneak out at night and go to Berea. There they saw even more people accept Jesus Christ.

When Paul moved to Athens, Silas and Timothy stayed behind but later joined him. Then they moved on to Corinth and began another church.

Silas can never be accused of leading a boring life. When he locked arms with Paul, one of life's greatest adventures was launched. Never did he dream he would be singing songs to God in jail in the middle of the night at Philippi. But he wouldn't have missed it for anything.

Something To Think About

1. What are the predominant personalities in your local church? Does it lean toward rigid or open? Are new people contributing to its growing awareness?
2. Have you ever accepted a teaching assignment you knew

you shouldn't? Can you think of a situation where damage has been done because someone refused to be quiet?

3. How do we account for Lydia's boldness? Are we too hesitant in our fellowship between men and women?

4. Are Christians good at accepting people who are different? Is your local church open enough to incorporate people with different backgrounds, economics and lifestyles?

5. What does Silas teach us about cheerfulness and depression?

6. Were Paul and Silas taking a foolish risk in refusing to be freed? Was it really their personal pride which insisted on a public display? The apostles must have made mistakes sometimes—was this one of them?

7. Wherever these missionary partners went, trouble seemed to follow. Are times better today for Christians? Are we better off with or without persecution?

11
MARK

He Grew in the Faith

Some people are rocks while others are rubber ducks. When we were children, most of us played in the bathtub with all sorts of paraphernalia. We tried to make bottle caps float on their backs. Then we would grab a small cardboard box and make a ship.

Whenever a bottle cap turned over or filled with water, it sank like a lead leaf. With rubber ducks it was different. We could hold them under the water, but whenever we let go, they shot back to the top.

John Mark was a rubber duck. People could get him down, even hold him there for awhile. But one thing you could count on—Mark would come back on top. Because of his buoyancy, this feisty disciple made one of the most lasting contributions in the history of Christendom.

Becoming discouraged is the normal Christian experience. Not the ideal, just the norm. The beginning of maturity is to realize how uneven life can be. Hopefully, as we develop, the drops become less sharp, less breathtaking and maybe less frequent. Nevertheless they still exist.

We shouldn't think that Jesus Christ was never discouraged or disappointed. When He counted on people the most, they often delivered the least. He must have been hurt by the lack of understanding from His disciples. Jesus taught them for three years and some days it seemed as if they had learned nothing.

John Mark is an interesting character who meets crushing defeat. The real story is in his ability to come back and regain the respect of everyone.

Mark was introduced beautifully to the Christian faith. His mother, Mary, had been involved in the early ministry with the disciples. We know nothing about his father, but Mark's mother opened her home to the disciples in Jerusalem (Acts 12:12).

When we meet Mary, King Herod was on the warpath. He had decided to put pressure on the growing Christian group. Ruthlessly, he had the apostle James murdered.

Peter was also arrested in the official crackdown and his future appeared shaky. Four guards were posted around the clock. Two were chained to the fisherman and two stood guard at the entrance. With the growing number of Christians, they weren't taking any chances on escape.

Naturally, the murderous situation sent fear rippling through the Christian community. The Jerusalem believers met in desperate, sincere prayer. They looked for God to do something and were claiming all the power of His promises (James 5:16).

Unknown to them, their prayers were answered in the positive. An angel of the Lord moved quietly into the prison, thumped Peter on the side, and led him to freedom. The whole operation was so slick the Rock thought it was all a dream. Once outside, the angel whisked away and left Peter on his own.

What does all of this have to do with John Mark? When Peter realized what had happened, he wanted to find the other Christians quickly. So the apostle took off directly for Mary's home. He knew the believers would be meeting there.

Despite rumors to the contrary, Mark was evidently not one of the original Christians. If he had met Jesus, it was only when he, John Mark, was a child. When Peter looked for Mary's house, it had been nearly fifteen years since the resurrection. Mark was to become one of those who had probably not seen and yet believed.

Mark saw the Christian faith under severe stress. He liked what he witnessed and at some time decided to believe for himself.

When Peter arrived at Mary's house, he knocked patiently at the door. Rhoda, the maid, answered the summons and was immediately flabbergasted. Leaving Peter at the gate, she ran back inside to tell the Christians. The believers called her crazy and insisted she had seen a ghost. But Peter kept steadily knocking until someone returned to let him in.

This is the type of Christianity Mark saw. Moments of enormous strength and fantastic faith, then acts of fickle uncertainty, self-doubt and near childishness. Later on, these inconsistencies might help him weather some devastating storms.

Herod executed the guards who were on duty— evidently he had trouble believing in angels. The Herod family was one of the most bloodthirsty clans in history, and this one finally died from worms. This passage is easy to date because history tells us Herod Agrippa died in A.D. 44.

As soon as the persecution died down, Paul and Barnabas brought relief supplies from Antioch to Jerusalem. In all probability they stayed at Mary's home. When they returned to Antioch, they took a new assistant with them named John Mark.

Mark was an intelligent man. We are all free to read the Gospel he wrote and see his ability. An intensely interested Christian, he began to collect information on the life of Christ. It is likely that he asked a multitude of questions from both Barnabas and Paul. They were not eyewitnesses to much of Jesus' ministry—possibly none; but they could share what they had been taught. The bulk of the material would come from Peter later.

It would be correct to picture Mark as a studious man. Eventually he compiled a book which necessitated careful details. It may be the first Life Of Christ ever written.

Luke, another excellent historian, tells us Mark served as an attendant on his journey with Paul and Barnabas. Literally, Mark was an "under-rower." He came along to help. The other two called the shots and made the major decisions. There is reason to believe the younger Christian was happy with the relationship.

The apostles had many uses for an assistant. Possibly he did little or no public speaking, but he could manage supplies, keep the treasury, locate lodging. Mark greased the wheels which kept the missionary enterprise rolling full force.

In our present day of glamour personalities,

Mark's position probably wouldn't sound too exciting. He drew no crowds and had no one who hung on his every word. A book on his life and conversion wouldn't stir many hearts or gather many shekels. Mark's name was more destined for a list of also-rans. But this did not in the least diminish his importance. He was a Christian standing in the gap where he felt God wanted him to stand.

Too often Christians put themselves down because they are "nobody." They seem to think God uses the same fame, wealth and star system we do. We use a *pressure structure* in the world. People are judged valuable on their ability to perform and produce. Those who do not succeed are useless. But when we become Christians, we often still use the same evaluation system.

God does not divide people into categories of important and unimportant. Only men keep this tally. He is no respecter of persons—we are all of equal value to Him. Some of us are too busy looking at other people's gifts to count our own (Romans 12:3-8).

Part of Mark's strength may have been that he was Barnabas' cousin (Colossians 4:10). Their fathers were possibly brothers. Consequently, Mark may have been selected for the first missionary journey on the basis of elementary nepotism. But don't knock the practice too hard. By choosing a relative, Barnabas may have avoided the trouble of an alien personality. This way they knew what they were getting into.

There may be a subtle but distinct leadership change as the missionary journey progresses. Barnabas had been Paul's mentor. He stood up for the former persecutor and introduced him to the fellowship. He stuck his neck out and was probably always glad he had. But as Paul grew spiritually, the new convert asserted himself more and now was running ahead. It is entirely possible that nothing could have made Barnabas happier. It appears a pleasant transition, without flak.

By coincidence, Mark began to withdraw his thinking from the other two. He changed his mind and decided to return to Jerusalem. Granted, it may have been a dastardly decision for Mark to make. Certainly Paul believed it was (Acts 15:38, 39). But in all fairness to the apostle, truth did not begin or end with him.

Over the long run it was probably good Mark left. For almost two thousand years it has furnished Christians with something to guess about. If we add it to the question of Paul's thorn, the salvation of Ananias and Sapphira and Cana wine, we have enough to ponder for two more millennia.

Was there a dispute over a doctrinal issue? Was Mark a dreamer with more time for theory than hard work? Whatever the problem, Paul's verdict was deep and painful. Mark could not go with them to the work (Acts 15:38). He refused to take Mark on the second missionary journey.

This was definitely a black mark against the young man's reputation. Paul was admired by many if not most. If word got out that the famous apostle had designated Mark as unfit, it would be a serious wound. Fortunately, Barnabas, a man of notable respect, came to his cousin's defense.

Now is the time to test Mark's resilience. He had been hit hard, fairly or not. What valid steps could he or should he take? Mark could start his own branch of Christianity. He wouldn't be the first or the last. Many organizations have begun not from the lofty spiritual goals their mail would have us believe, but from some disgruntled number-two men who have launched out on their own tangent.

Most of our great historical divisions have not come over deep doctrinal issues. One denomination split over the question of whether to publish a magazine. Another group parted ways over whether to allow their pastors to wear beards. In the first century, matters were often just as silly. A local congregation was at each other's throats over which missionaries to entertain (III John). Some were ferocious over circumcision and pork (Acts 15).

From what mettle is Mark made? Will he defend himself by carrying out a gossip campaign against Paul? Will he drive a wedge so deeply it can never be repaired? Serious issues for a young and growing faith; they had enough enemies on the outside without spouting fangs among their members.

Two years after the incident occurred the Mark issue was still hot for Paul. We don't know how Mark felt, but when Paul proposed a second missionary journey, Barnabas volunteered Mark. Paul soured immediately and refused to accept Barnabas' cousin. There would be no healing. The apostle couldn't bring himself to trust Mark again.

Barnabas split with Paul and took Mark on his own missionary journey. This is the last we hear of John Mark for some time. Not just months pass by or even years, but a decade slips by before we again find a trace of his name.

Perhaps he led a life of outstanding service. For,

during those ten years, something significant changed in Mark's life. The next time we find his name is in a letter written by Paul. The apostle described his setting and listed his companions. Paul was imprisoned in Rome, and one of his fellow prisoners was a man named Mark (Colossians 4:10; Philemon 24).

Whatever rough edges had developed between the two, events over the years had apparently smoothed them out. Maybe Mark had a serious change of heart and admitted he had been wrong twelve years before. Or possibly Paul asked forgiveness from his former assistant.

A Christian psychologist once gave especially good advice at a seminar concerning broken relationships. He told us to never tell someone, "I don't ever want to talk to you again." Doors have to be left open. Even in the harshest of hostilities, room has to be made for healing. Pity the poor parent who says, "If you marry her we never want to see you again." These are strong words which are hard to forget.

There was no doubt the relationship had come full cycle when Paul wrote his second letter to Timothy, for he asked Timothy to bring Mark with him "for he is profitable to me for the ministry" (II Timothy 4:11). Their Christian faith was vibrant.

Not only had Mark been reunited with Paul, but his sphere of service had grown enormously. Somehow he became acquainted with Peter. Not just casually, but they had developed a strong mutual respect. When Peter wrote his first epistle he ended it by sending a greeting from Mark (I Peter 5:13). The warmth of this relationship is obvious when Peter calls him "my son." The famous fisherman had enormous respect and affection for the veteran missionary.

It has been twenty years since we first met Mark at his mother's house in Jerusalem. He has weathered some storms. Doubtless many more than we are aware of. Still he is commended for his faith and service. He is well known among the churches and evidently well thought of. His name is mentioned by both Peter and Paul because they knew it would light a candle for those who heard it.

Thanks, Mark, for pulling through. We don't know if it was your fault or Paul's. Maybe it was just a mutual misunderstanding. But we are glad you bounced back. It will encourage all of us when we take a stunning blow.

Something To Think About

1. Do the Christians you know have their ups and downs? What things discourage you? Is there a noticeable pattern?
2. How do you look at prayer? Why do we pray? Have you ever prayed for a miracle and received it? Explain.
3. Is there much jealousy among Christian workers? Explain. Where there is jealousy, what is its cause?
4. What effect do famous Christian "personalities" have on the church? Do you think their long-range effect is helpful or demoralizing?
5. In your opinion, who was probably right—Paul, Barnabas or Mark?
6. Do you see good harmony among Christians? Explain.
7. What is the biggest hindrance to reconciliation? Why do people hold grudges so long?

12
PAUL
Part I

Zealous and Forthright, He Inspired Passion In Others

When we mention brave missionaries, we usually imagine Livingstone trekking across the dark African continent. But there is one Christian hero who gets too little attention. His name is Ananias. God asked him to go and meet a murderer of Christians. Sometimes I envy the missionaries in Hawaii or Jamaica, but I have never wanted to trade places with Ananias.

The executioner's name was Saul of Tarsus—also called Paul. This Pharisee was probably the least likely prospect for conversion in the civilized world. His hate for the church of Christ could only be measured astronomically.

Paul was a man of total dedication. No matter which side he was on, he gave it everything. It is hard to picture him as moody. Occasionally he may have basked in self-pity, but seldom. At times Paul was lonely and said so. Most of the time he came across as having it all together and being self-contained.

The apostle is easily identified as a person of notable intelligence. Anyone can read his letters and see good organization and clarity. Many of the Christian concepts we banter around today, Paul first enunciated with precision. We can all be grateful he was Christianity's first great scholar.

Paul was also personable. In most locations he attracted people. His delivery, sincerity and logic were compelling. More than one adversary accepted Christ after hearing this man.

Despite his tremendous talents and abilities, this great man managed to stay in the human race. Some people hated him totally. They worked hard at keeping him humble. The church members at Corinth and other places weren't bashful about expressing their hostilities.

Paul forded many streams and climbed hundreds of steep mountains. He wasn't always right. But he was always dedicated. God had selected an outstanding pacesetter.

Just before Ananias met Paul, the Terror from Tarsus had just completed a campaign to eliminate Christians (Acts 9:1). In the process Jesus Christ interrupted his life. The road to Damascus was the sight of a miraculous vision which completely transformed the anti-Christian. In humility a proud determined man bowed his heart before the risen Lord. He would no longer resist a compassionate God.

The trip Paul was making before his conversion was a good indication of his zeal. Damascus was 120 miles northeast of Jerusalem—probably a good six-day walk each way. His plans were to arrest Christians who had sought refuge in Syria. There was a sizeable population of both Jews and Christians living there. He and his cohorts were going to bind and return them to a Jerusalem jail.

Christians were then called people of "the Way" (Acts 16:17; 18:26; 19:9, 23; 22:4; 24:14, 22). They earned this title because Christ referred to Himself as "the way" in John 14:6. Believers were later named Christians at Antioch.

After his dramatic vision, Paul was led sightless into Damascus. There he remained for three days and nights without eating or drinking.

Enter our hero—Ananias. After no small debate, God convinced him it was safe to visit this monster. The Lord had a special plan and wanted to use Paul to convert Gentiles. Ananias went (probably without enthusiasm) to the home of Judas on Straight Street. There he found a tame Paul, completely de-clawed.

Ananias put his hands on Paul and his sight was returned. Paul arose and was immediately baptized. Local believers at Damascus welcomed their old persecutor like a rich uncle.

This event must be ranked with the most important ones to ever happen in Christian history. Naturally all believers are of equal value before God. Yet, this conversion helped tremendously to catapult the new faith to a soaring position. If Peter caused Christianity to race, Paul taught it to fly.

Paul was immediately enthusiastic and began preaching in the Damascus synagogues. When he became more bold in his preaching, the Jews became hostile. They decided the turncoat would have to die. When his new Christian friends heard about it, they helped Paul escape Damascus by lowering him over the wall in a basket (Acts 9:25).

It genuinely bothers me to see Paul on the wall.

What happened to the man who could do anything? Had his faith failed him? Paul, go back and stare those renegades in the eyes and impress them with your courage! Paul on a wall, indeed!

But thanks for climbing it. All of us are encouraged to know there is a time to quit. Some situations are hopeless. Yet we often act as if it is a disgrace to back off. As if it were a moral corrosion if we pronounced something as irretrievable.

Some people have wasted years pursuing empty clouds. There was nothing there, but they wouldn't admit it. More than one class would have flourished if the teacher had had enough sense to move on.

We are glad Paul wasn't playing the hero in a grade B movie. He knew when to quit and head for the wall. We are all better off because he hid in a basket.

Paul then took off for Jerusalem. He had high hopes of joining the other Christian disciples.

Before he arrived, the disciples called the meeting off. They didn't know what kind of trick this was, but they wanted no part of it. Paul was a murderer who would sell his own mother to kill Christians. They voted to reject his invitation to meet—all of this despite the lapse of three years since his conversion (Galatians 1:18).

The scene is reminiscent of Charles Colson and the Watergate era. He had a gruesome reputation as a White House henchman. Several commentators referred to him as a man without conscience.

When Colson became a Christian, many people scoffed. He was up to tricks. The crook was trying to get off with a lighter sentence. The convicted lawyer had to take time to prove himself by both words and actions. Some Christians accepted him readily and shouldered the risk. Others were cautious and suspicious. Maybe a few have never believed his conversion. Fortunately, a handful of close Christian friends ran to his side like a moth to a light.

The same thing happened to Paul. Ananias, Barnabas and a collection of believers at Damascus took the risk and befriended him. They are to be heralded as the noblest of believers.

Once in awhile a Christian gets burned in befriending others. But that's the chance we must be willing to take because we love.

After Barnabas spoke out for Paul, the disciples agreed to go along with him and a fantastic brother was gained. Paul had not shared his testimony for long before the Greek Jews also wanted to kill him. The tentmaker must have felt like Custer at the Little Big Horn. The Jews didn't trust him. The Greek Jews wanted to murder him. The Christians were keeping an eye on the novice. Becoming a believer was no easy thing. He finally decided the best thing to do was to return to Tarsus. Maybe time would clear the smoke and heal the wounds.

With the conversion of Paul, the persecution of the church dwindled to dust. It would be hard to exaggerate the terror he had leveled on the early believers. He had raised havoc on the church (Acts 8:3). Now no one was more responsible for the peace and prosperity of the same institution. Its members were suddenly safe because Paul was one of them (Acts 9:31).

The controversy over the apostle's name seems endless. Its solution is probably simple. He always had both names, Saul and Paul. His Jewish friends had called him Saul. When he became a missionary to the Gentiles, most people used the more popular Paul. It was no more complicated than this (Acts 13:9).

If the church was at relative peace, it was not idle. New groups of believers were popping up everywhere. One group was at Antioch. When the leaders at Jerusalem heard of the body, they sent Barnabas to check it out. He was so impressed he went to Tarsus to collect his old friend Paul, and the two spent a full year working with the new Christians. Paul was in high gear.

An enormous famine covered the Roman Empire during the reign of Claudius. The Christians at Antioch responded to the crisis by sending relief to those hard-pressed in Jerusalem. Paul had the privilege of going with Barnabas on this mission of love (Acts 11:28-30).

Paul wore many hats during his Christian adventures. Sometimes he settled down and pastored for a couple of years. At other times he was an extensive author. Few things pleased him more than the role of teacher. For years Paul traveled as a dedicated missionary.

His checkered and colorful career led him to tremendous variety. He would not have been happy with some views held by many today. There is often a pressure applied which insists, "once a pastor, always a pastor." If a missionary doesn't return to the field, he had better have a bad back, or else we think he has suffered a moral crisis.

What would we have thought of Paul? A rover at best. He hung loose and mobile. If he felt led to abandon this project and pursue that one, he charged ahead. He couldn't become paralyzed worrying whether others would understand.

A large part of Paul's time was spent as a missionary. Years of it was spent on the road visiting cities. His first full-fledged tour began at the suggestion of the church at Antioch.

Theirs was a fascinating concept in missionary selection. The elders of a local church approached two consecrated Christians and asked them to become missionaries. The church in turn pledged prayer (Acts 13:1-4).

This may be a vast improvement over some of our present practices. Usually we put the major pressure on the person who wants to become a missionary. Under the system at Antioch the church took the initiative. They went to the potential candidate and told him how they felt the Spirit was leading.

Talk about a confidence builder! Paul and Barnabas must have felt like they were hang gliding. The trials they would face were bad enough. At least they were assured of the boost of knowing the church was fully behind them. Maybe more contemporary churches should go back to the same practice.

Paul's first missionary journey was a swing across the island of Cyprus and a tour into lower Asia Minor (Acts 13; 14). A number were in the party, including Barnabas and John Mark.

One of the most dramatic events which occurred on the trip came early at Paphos on Cyprus. As with all their stops, the people were dedicated to paganism. They worshipped the goddess called "The Paphian," a Syrian deity.

While here the local procounsul, Sergius Paulus, asked to see them because he was intrigued with the gospel. The apostles responded but they encountered harsh opposition. Bar-Jesus (also called Elymas), a local witch-doctor/magician, blocked their way, trying to keep them from the official.

Paul wasted no time with the quack and by the power of God cast a darkness on Bar-Jesus (Acts 13:11). While his friends led him away, the missionary delivered the good news, and the net result was the conversion of the proconsul.

The presence of God in Paul's ministry was obvious. They were ready to meet all other powers head-on. Their next stop was Perga, where John Mark left the entourage. Afterwards they proceeded to another Antioch—this one located at Pisidia.

As was often the case, the missionaries visited the synagogue and were invited to speak to the congregation. Paul's presentation of the gospel was clear and moving. A large segment of the people wanted to hear more and the next Saturday almost the entire city showed up to hear Paul.

This type of response got some people jumping mad. But the angrier they became, the more determinedly Paul roared his message. A gospel of grace and forgiveness was being preached to both Jews and Gentiles but as far as some were concerned, it was worse than paganism.

Crowds gathered to harass the men and soon they were forced out of the city. The apostles shook the dust off their feet and headed for the next town. This was an old symbol of contempt. Some believe it to be a literal gesture, and it may have been. If so, a person and his party stopped with great fanfare and removed their sandals. With great drama they raised each one and shook the dust clear. Anyone watching would have known they had been insulted.

Christ taught His disciples to do this whenever their audience was hostile (Matthew 10:11-14). Whether He meant it literally or figuratively can be debated until the dandelions march off the lawn.

The missionaries continued to hopscotch across Asia Minor. At Iconium a number believed—the rest drove them out of town. They preached extensively in the Derbe and Lystra areas. In Lystra Paul healed a man who had never before walked. The populace was amazed at this indisputable miracle (Acts 14:11). Because of their pagan backgrounds, the people assumed Paul and his friends were gods. They called Barnabas Jupiter, and Paul Mercurius. The only way to treat a deity was to worship it, but the Christians loudly declined the honor.

Fame is a fleeting folly. Before long some men tried to stone the missionaries and nearly succeeded. Paul was assaulted and thrown outside the gates, presumed dead. He revived and the next day was able to travel to Derbe.

Often we see a missionary journey as lines on a map. They went from city A to city B to city C. In reality those tours were less rifle and more shotgun. They backtracked, spread out into the countryside, spent weeks here, months there, and sometimes years in various places. They weren't on a promotion tour. They were going everywhere they thought they could get in. The missionaries tried to leave a lasting ministry in each area. They appointed elders to watch over the work after they moved on.

When Paul returned to Antioch, he gave a report to his home church. God had worked miracles and opened the gospel to the Gentiles. Paul and Barnabas then took time out to attend the monumental council at Jerusalem (Acts 15). Their testimony was of considerable value in giving full stature to converted Gentiles.

Soon the zeal to share was rising in their blood again. Paul and Barnabas decided to revisit those areas where they had preached before. Barnabas and Paul debated taking John Mark with them since he had left during the last trip. Paul refused, so Barnabas split and took Mark with him. Paul may have been wrong. He then selected Silas.

Paul's second missionary journey took him thousands of miles. He and Silas picked up Timothy along the route and he also had Luke along. Some of the highlights of the trip were Philippi, Thessalonica, Athens and Corinth.

At Philippi Paul and Silas sang at night in prison (Acts 16:25). Before they were finished, the jailer had become a repentant Christian.

Their next stop was Thessalonica. They saw many converts and started an excellent church. As with several other cities, they had to sneak out at night.

At Athens, Paul preached his famous sermon on Mars' Hill. The story of the resurrection received mixed reviews. Some received it eagerly, while others merely rocked back and forth and had a good laugh (Acts 17:32).

The fourth major event happened at Corinth. The good news was delivered first to the Jews of the city. They vetoed it, so Paul, Silas and Timothy turned to the Gentiles. Justus and Crispus, a ruler of the synagogue, accepted Jesus as the Messiah, and God asked Paul to stay in Corinth. He continued to work with them for a year and a half.

On the way home Paul visited Cenchrea, Ephesus

and Caesarea. At Cenchrea Paul shaved his head and took a vow (Acts 18:18). We don't know why he did this. He was greatly moved by something, probably. It is possible he shaved his head twice—once when he made the vow and again when it was completed. Our hair grows at the rate of 5 to 5½ inches a year, so Paul must have spent months with little more than a fuzzy layer.

It must have been a warm reunion when Paul returned to Antioch. Christian friendships often run deep. Those who had been encouraging from the beginning held a particularly special place.

God was not done using the converted Pharisee, however. After he had spent some time at Antioch, Paul launched out on his third missionary journey. This tour would again take the apostle for thousands of miles. Those of us with cars may find it difficult to appreciate what these trips meant. Normally, the foot was the only means of transportation. Sometimes a cart passed by, but the rider soon wished he was back on foot. The best method was by ship, but of course there were only so many places ships could go.

At Ephesus Paul found believers who knew only John's baptism. They had heard about the Messiah, but their knowledge was spotty. The apostle helped them and they were baptized in the name of Christ. When Paul laid his hands on them they received the Holy Spirit and spoke in tongues (Acts 19:6). Their experience matched those of Pentecost, the Samaritan and Cornelius.

Paul tried to preach in the synagogues, but after three months was driven out. He then moved into the building which housed the school of Tyrannus. This became his preaching center for two years. News spread all over Asia Minor about the fantastic ministry which took place there.

The miracles Paul performed at Ephesus were startling. He exorcised demons. That would seem a noble endeavor, but in most pagan communities the citizens had made peace with the demons. They understood each other and learned to compromise. Ephesus was one of those bedfellows.

When locals became Christians, they abandoned their idols and gave up paganism. Those who made the idols and trinkets found that hard to appreciate. The silversmiths became angry enough to kill Paul (Acts 19:29) and his companions.

After the uproar Paul and his party left for Macedonia. In Troas a man named Eutychus was sitting in a window listening to Paul preach. The young man fell asleep and tumbled three floors to his death, and the apostle brought him back to life. His relatives can be found in the back pews of churches to this day.

Paul went to Miletus, then swung toward Ephesus to meet with the elders there. When he had given them final instructions and started to leave, the leaders hugged him and kissed his neck. They knew they probably would not see him again (Acts 20:37, 38).

When Paul arrived at Tyre, disciples tried to talk him out of going to Jerusalem, but the apostle was determined and could not be dissuaded.

While Paul was readying for the trip to Jerusalem a prophet named Agabus came over from Judea. With tremendous drama the prophet took off Paul's girdle (a waist cloth which pulled his clothes together) and tied it around Paul's hands and feet. Then he warned Paul that if he went to Jerusalem, the Gentiles would capture him (Acts 21:11).

Did this prophecy mean that God did not want Paul to go to Jerusalem? Not necessarily. The prophet never interprets the prophecy; he merely states the facts. If Paul were to go he would be arrested. It didn't mean he shouldn't go; God may have simply been giving him the option to turn around.

Some believe Paul was clearly wrong to go. He could have been. It was within his capability. But he also may have been as right as at any time in his life. The consequences were sizable: A long imprisonment awaited Paul, and the church would be robbed of a tremendous missionary.

His friends thought the apostle was wrong to go. They wept and begged him to stay. Paul assured them that prison meant relatively little. If necessary, he was quite willing to die for the name of Christ.

At this point Paul's friends came on like a blanket in a snowstorm. They did not agree with Paul's decision. Each had their say. They talked, wept, reasoned and argued. But Paul couldn't be changed one iota. So they dropped the subject and offered 100 percent backing. The apostle really knew how to pick friends.

Compare this with those who lay down ultimatums. A parent tells his grown son, "If you do it that way don't ever ask me for advice again." A mother says, "If you marry him, I won't come to the wedding."

Where is the compassion? What happens to tolerance? A Christian friend is someone who loves the people he disagrees with. Conditional love is manipulating. When your son disobeys you, he remains your son. Christ had compassion for the people who didn't accept Him.

We would become more creative, more daring if we were sure our Christian friends would back us. They don't have to agree—just love.

Something To Think About

1. Are we too cautious of accepting new converts? Or are we too casual about accepting them?
2. Can you think of mistakes made because someone didn't quit in time? Have you experienced this?
3. Did the disciples have a right to hold off on Paul? Should they have met with him immediately?
4. Have you seen a Christian befriended as Ananias and Barnabas did Paul? Explain.
5. Do we look down on Christians who give up "full time ministries"? Have some missionaries you have known suffered this way?
6. Do you know any Christians who could be approached about becoming missionaries? Would the system of church leaders taking the initiative work in your group?
7. Do we support Christians we do not agree with? Are we too concerned with harmony among our friends?

13
PAUL
Part II

Moving Forward Always, He Followed The Vision Of Christ

Whenever you try to please everyone, the ceiling is bound to cave in. Paul had the highest ideals—if there were any way to keep everyone happy, he would find that route. But sometimes it backfired and the apostle got burned.

His predicament is similar to that of every Christian. There is a gentle tension which makes us want to please each other. We know by Scripture and experience we have no right to offend people. In fact, Paul was the major architect of the principle. He wrote this guideline to the church at Corinth: "For though I be free from all men, yet have I made myself servant unto all, that I might gain the more" (I Corinthians 9:19).

Despite our noblest intentions we can't keep everyone pleased. There comes a point at which we must draw the line and merely do it our way. Paul's eagerness to avoid waves resulted in agonizing confinement.

When the apostle arrived in Jerusalem, he told the local Jewish Christians of the miracles happening among the Gentiles. His report received mixed reviews. Consequently, the elders reached a compromise aimed at pleasing everyone. Paul needed to do something to prove he had not abandoned Judaism. According to the plan this would enamor the Jewish Christians on both sides.

Fortunately, as they saw it, the opportunity was knocking at their door. Four men were going to the temple to take Jewish vows of purification. If Paul joined them in the ceremony and paid part of the tab, Jews everywhere would be thrilled.

The plan sounded good to Paul. But if he had known what was waiting, the apostle might have caught the next cart for Asia Minor.

A riot broke out in the courts. Some men recognized Paul during the ceremonies and complained loudly. To them he was the Jewish Christian who was teaching blasphemy against the Old Testament. They also charged he had an Ephesian named Trophimus with him in the temple, a clear violation of temple law.

In all likelihood, this latter charge was only a heated rumor. When people get angry they will shout anything. Members of the crowd knew the Gentile was a friend of Paul's, but they probably didn't see Trophimus in the temple.

It was an irresponsible act on the part of the crowd. We should all be reminded of the blindness of hate. Even the coolest heads do irrational and cruel things under these circumstances.

We see hate at its blindest in the crucifixion of Christ. He was killed over the basest of instincts.

Jesus knew he had been delivered up because of envy (Matthew 27:18). A major factor in destruction is often runaway passion.

The crowd swelled in number instantly. Those who were shouting absurdities were persuasive. Not that crowds are particularly discerning at best; they are traditionally followers and not thinkers. The large group pressed in on Paul immediately. They grabbed him and brutally dragged him out of the temple. It was now an unruly mob who started beating on the apostle with enough force to kill him.

Paul's death would have been certain if someone hadn't intervened. An unknown volunteer (maybe the modest Luke) ran to summon the Roman guards. Just northwest of the temple, Roman troops were housed at a fortress called Antonia. They were located close to the temple for the specific purpose of controlling crowds.

At least 200 soldiers came pouring out of the garrison. Without hesitation they shot down the steps which led directly to the temple. The sight of running soldiers so frightened the cowardly crowd they fairly evaporated.

Unable to figure out right away what was wrong, the Roman captain bound Paul in chains. Everyone was hurling accusations, only adding to the confusion. The captain decided to arrest the apostle until he could clear the problem.

As Paul was lifted up the stairs he asked if he could be allowed to address the crowd. The captain consented, and silence came over the noisy group.

Paul used this opportunity to give his testimony. Step by step he explained who he was and how he had become a Christian (Acts 22:1-21).

The crowd may have been somewhat restless, but they listened up to a point. But when Paul reminded them of his mission to the Gentiles, they again ignited. They reacted now like frustrated children. Clothes were torn, dust was thrown into the air, oaths and pleas were screamed in despair. Paul's speech had not gone over well.

To protect him and to further the examination, the captain had Paul taken inside the castle. Just in case it might help uncover the truth, Paul was to be beaten. The Romans used a whip with leather strips, each piece studded with metal, bone or stones. It wasn't uncommon to have someone die under this torture. The guards didn't care.

Under Roman law a citizen could not be beaten without a fair trial. Paul considered this a good time to bring up the subject of his citizenship.

The appointed beaters immediately walked away. They weren't about to beat a Roman citizen; the penalties were too severe for breaking this law.

Instead, the captain kept Paul under arrest until he could hear the arguments against him. He commanded the chief priests to show up for the inquisition.

During the inquiry Paul pulled off a cool ploy. Half the Sanhedrin consisted of Pharisees and the other half were Sadducees. All the apostle had to do was mention the resurrection. In a second the two parties were fighting each other, debating the resurrection. Finally the Pharisees found Paul innocent. The Sadducees threw a fit. The chief captain, afraid the apostle would be torn apart, returned Paul to the fort.

That night the Lord appeared to Paul. He wanted to assure him everything was all right. The turmoil in

Jerusalem had a purpose. Because of it Paul would testify of Christ in the city of Rome (Acts 23:11). This had to be a great comfort to the spinning apostle, and the timing was excellent. If ever Paul needed a lift, it must have been then.

If God gave the apostle peace, his enemies were determined not to. Forty of them pooled their anger and decided to kill Paul. They pledged to not eat or drink until the rebel was silenced forever (Acts 23:12-15). Their conspiracy needed cooperation from the Sanhedrin. The plan was to have Paul brought out for further questioning. They would then finish him off.

At this point an interesting character enters the story. He is identified as the son of Paul's sister. We don't know how he heard of the plot. It is obvious from the argument at the Sanhedrin that the apostle had some friends there. The nephew is merely a shadow who moves quietly in and out. He certainly risked his life by bringing the news to Paul. The gang of hostile assassins would think nothing of erasing this young life also.

When Paul heard of the plot he instantly called for one of the centurions and had him take his nephew to see the captain. The soldier had no trouble believing the youth's story of the plot to take Paul and kill him. He sent him home and summoned two centurions.

The captain literally called out the army. He asked for an escort of 470 men. This included 200 heavily armed soldiers, 70 horsemen and 200 spearmen (Acts 23:23). There would be no unnecessary chances. These figures are entirely feasible since the captain had at least 1,000 men under his command.

Paul was to be delivered post haste to Caesarea, 60 miles away. There he was to be taken directly to Felix the governor. We don't know how the apostle felt about the separation of church and state. However, we are left with no doubts about his feelings on the separation of head and shoulders. Paul was grateful for military assistance. He knew what the soldiers didn't. This journey wouldn't end until he finally arrived in Rome. God had already punched his ticket.

Felix was the governor of Judea as appointed by Rome. He helps date our chapter because history tells us he ruled from A.D. 52-60. Josephus, the historian, depicts Felix as a harsh ruler, not to be trusted. The Jews sent a special delegation to Rome to have the despot removed, but his powerful brother, Pallas, protected him.

Felix decided to keep Paul until his adversaries could come from Jerusalem. He may have been less concerned with fairness to Paul than with the safety of his own neck. His previous adventures made him shy of offending the Jews unnecessarily. Meanwhile Paul would rest in Herod's judgment hall.

Five days later a group from Jerusalem arrived to state their case against the Christian. (If the henchmen left behind were keeping their vow, they hadn't eaten for days. They may have been unhappy but doubtless they looked trim and neat.) Ananias joined the party and Tertullus was brought along as chief spokesman or lawyer.

Tertullus stated his case with great flattery. He thanked Felix for the peace which existed in the territory. A not-too-subtle hint that if tranquility was to prevail, a favorable ruling would be wise (Acts 24:2).

Felix then invited Paul to reply to the charges presented. The apostle gave a brief background of the problem and then cut to its heart. The real reason he was there was his teaching of the resurrection.

Paul's words were not wasted on the governor. Felix had already been told of the Christian "Way." We don't know exactly how, but there were many possibilities. Thousands of people were now witnessing. Maybe the message had even impressed his third wife, Drusilla. At any rate he wanted to hear more. In the meantime he would send for Lysias, the captain in Jerusalem.

While they waited, Felix decided to have a private audience with Paul. He and his wife (who was Jewish) listened to the apostle explain the "Way" further. Felix was engrossed with what he heard. The teaching was practical and ethical. These were concepts not often discussed in pagan circles. Felix shook at some of the things he heard.

But Felix's interests were torn in too many directions. He wanted to hear the truth but his conflicts were legion. The governor would also like to make some gold on the deal; he wanted Paul to bribe him. This was the way he was accustomed to operating. He would also like to see the Jews pacified. In all of this Felix needed to keep the lid on Rome. It was similar to trying to ride four horses at once. There was no way to handle them all well.

Still hoping to have his cake and eat it, Felix dismissed Paul and said they would visit again. He becomes the classic example of procrastination. The governor had been confronted head-on with the truth and decided to dodge it. He becomes the genuine relative of us all.

It was easy to sidestep the issue day by day. Most of us don't enjoy making decisions. Maybe Felix was hoping for a special light to break in. If he released Paul, his enemies would be inflamed. Should he keep the apostle, his conscience might continue to stir. Then there was the matter of the money he hoped to get.

Meanwhile, weeks turned into months and months to years. After two years Felix was relieved of his job. And still he had not solved the Paul problem. With one last procrastination Felix decided to leave the apostle for his successor to handle. No sense making anyone mad.

The assurance Paul received from God must have meant a great deal by now. The lonely nights in jail would have been enough to try anyone's faith.

Festus became the new governor. He didn't even have his tunics unpacked before the Paul issue came up. The religious leaders in Jerusalem asked to have the rebel sent to Jerusalem—still planning to lay in wait and ambush Paul. (Those religious leaders must have been tired from not eating all this time!)

The new governor refused and invited members of the Sanhedrin to appear for a new trial. They came, hate still bellowing like a dragon with heartburn.

After listening to the accusations, Festus came up with a surprise. Why not send Paul back to Jerusalem for his trial? How the renegades got him to agree to this is still a mystery. Fortunately, Paul was too alert to fall for their treachery.

He protested and appealed to Caesar (25:10). He fully recognized Rome's control over him and the apostle was willing to accept it. Even execution was within Caesar's authority. But Paul had no plans to be murdered by a mob.

The apostle had no hesitancy about using the civil courts. God had put them into power to protect the people (Romans 13). He taught it, believed it and used them.

Festus didn't seem a bit disturbed. He wasn't sure how he got into this mess, but he was happy to get out. If a Roman citizen appealed to Caesar, who was he to deny it? Paul could catch the next boat out as far as Festus was concerned.

At this point, King Herod Agrippa and his wife, Bernice, came to Caesarea to greet the new governor. The entire family of Herod consisted of immoral cut-throats. Each member of the throne had murdered to keep his position secure.

Festus told the Judean king about the apostle and the circumstances surrounding his arrest. Agrippa decided he would like to meet the man. The next day the king and his wife entered the meeting hall with pretentious pomp, and after a short introduction Paul was called on by Agrippa to speak.

Paul gave an excellent explanation of his faith (Acts 26). He described his Jewish heritage with pride. The apostle depicted his role as persecutor of the church. Then, with moving drama, Paul outlined the miracle which brought him to Christ on the road to Damascus and directly challenged the king.

Paul's plea was compassionate. This was no simple request to join a lodge. He wasn't asking the king to go fishing with the boys. It was an invitation to be reconciled with the Living God through Jesus Christ.

Festus wasn't impressed—he considered Paul insane and said so. Evidently Agrippa wasn't thrilled either. He virtually said, "With this little argument you expect to persuade me?" (26:28, paraphrase). It is really a statement of derision rather than agreement. Agrippa had too much at stake to jump ship now. One didn't give up everything that easily and become a Christian. Maybe men like Matthew and Peter could walk away from everything. But kings didn't do that. Christ would hold no claim on *his* life.

Festus and Agrippa went off to discuss the question of Paul's imprisonment. Whatever his religious problem, he had done nothing to justify incarceration. As Agrippa said, they could have set him free if he had not appealed to Caesar.

The apostle probably wasn't too rattled by the decision. He never doubted he was going to Rome. If the trip was going to be slow, he would have all the more time to spread the gospel.

Paul was delivered to a centurion for his historical trip to Italy. The soldier's name was Julius of the Augustus band. Several prisoners were scheduled to sail across the Mediterranean.

Julius was a considerate man—practically all the centurions in the New Testament are. When the ship docked at Sidon after one day at sea, Paul was allowed to leave the vessel. There he met with friends and recharged spiritually and emotionally before sailing again.

If Julius was a kind man, this unlikely friendship also speaks well of Paul. The apostle attracted other people. His manner and personality often won the day for him.

At Alexandria they switched ships in favor of one heading for Italy. When they set sail again, a wind greeted them and forced the vessel to go south of the island of Crete.

The ship's captain wanted to get started before the winds grew worse. But Paul warned that the voyage would only result in damage to the vessel and the loss of life. Julius finally agreed with the captain and they struck out again across the uneasy sea. Winter would be hard in their present port so they decided to risk moving. They sailed close to the shoreline.

Suddenly a gigantic storm arose. Experienced sailors called it the Euroclydon because it came from the northeast. There was considerable concern that the vessel might break apart.

Hurriedly they began tying cables around the hull to stop the boards from coming apart with the wind and water pressure. But the next day they still feared for their lives and started throwing things overboard—equipment, luggage, almost anything they could do without. They had every reason to believe they were staring death in the eye.

After several desperate days, Paul talked to the crew and passengers. He reminded them of his warning not to leave the harbor. (He couldn't help but get that in.) Now they would be wise to listen. God had guaranteed Paul safe passage to Rome. All they had to do was stay with the ship.

On the fourteenth night the ship was driven near land. When the crew believed they were about to crash, they prepared to abandon ship. Paul quickly pleaded with the centurion that if the men did not stay with the vessel they would die.

Julius was a man of decision; he moved swiftly to cut the ropes, releasing the sideboat. Now no one could leave.

The ship held 276 people. Paul encouraged them to eat, and after they had they felt better about the situation. But there was still work to do so they started throwing the wheat cargo overboard. They then lifted the anchors and hoped the wind would drive them into a small creek with a shore.

When the ship hit the shore the back broke up from the violent waves. The soldiers wanted to move quickly to kill the prisoners, but again Paul prevailed by talking to the centurion. They all abandoned the splintered vessel and held on to floating boards. Everyone was able to reach shore safely as Paul had predicted.

They recognized their island refuge as Melita (28:1). The inhabitants did not have the same culture or language as the Greeks and Romans. Consequently, the islanders were considered barbarians by the crew. It was the usual superiority complex. We often look at people who are different as automatically inferior.

But their behavior was far from barbarian. They kindled a fire for their sudden visitors, which was greatly appreciated. The cold, wet and wind were making them miserable.

As Paul gathered wood, a snake bit him on the arm. The people of Melita assumed he was a murderer or other vicious criminal—otherwise the viper would not have bitten him. Paul merely shook off the snake and went about his business. Everyone waited for him to swell up and die, but he was fine.

When the chief's father was sick almost to death, Paul laid hands on the elderly man. Instantly he was healed. Publius, the chief, gave great honor to the entire party because of the miracle.

They stayed at Melita for three months before resuming their trip. In Rome the prisoners, except for Paul, were delivered to the prison. He was kept separately, with a private guard. The apostle was probably chained to the guard's arm.

Paul never lost his bearings despite the hardships. His job was primarily that of a witness to the power of Jesus Christ.

The apostle spent two years in Rome. The authorities allowed him to live under house arrest, so he rented a home. During that time he fulfilled the job God had for him. Paul was a short-term missionary to the people of Italy.

Luke tells us Paul preached with confidence and no one tried to stop him (Acts 28:31).

Something To Think About

1. Do you feel a pressure to try to please everyone? Have we taken this too far?
2. What are some sick effects of hate? How does it blind judgment?
3. Was Paul wrong in pleading his case to a pagan army? Can Christian workers expect the government to protect them?
4. Paul's nephew took great risk in warning Paul. Can you think of any quiet but brave Christians?
5. Some men do cruel things in the name of their faith. Can you think of some?
6. Paul was treated badly by leaders who procrastinated. Can you think of times when people have been hurt because others refused to make decisions?
7. Did you accept Christ quickly or after much indecision? Why did you do it the way you did?